Realizing the Potential of Interorganizational Cooperation

Hal Beder, *Editor*

NEW DIRECTIONS FOR CONTINUING EDUCATION
GORDON DARKENWALD, ALAN B. KNOX, *Editors-in-Chief*

Number 23, September 1984

Paperback sourcebooks in
The Jossey-Bass Higher Education Series

Jossey-Bass Inc., Publishers
San Francisco • Washington • London

LC
5215
.R42

Hal Beder (Ed.).
Realizing the Potential of Interorganizational Cooperation.
New Directions for Continuing Education, no. 23.
San Francisco: Jossey-Bass, 1984.

New Directions for Continuing Education Series
Gordon G. Darkenwald, Alan B. Knox, *Editors-in-Chief*

Copyright © 1984 by Jossey-Bass Inc., Publishers
and
Jossey-Bass Limited

Copyright under International, Pan American, and Universal
Copyright Conventions. All rights reserved. No part of
this issue may be reproduced in any form—except for brief
quotation (not to exceed 500 words) in a review or professional
work—without permission in writing from the publishers.

New Directions for Continuing Education (publication number
USPS 493-930) quarterly by Jossey-Bass Inc., Publishers.
Second-class postage rates paid at San Francisco, California,
and at additional mailing offices.

Correspondence:
Subscriptions, single-issue orders, change of address notices, undelivered
copies, and other correspondence should be sent to Subscriptions,
Jossey-Bass Inc., Publishers, 433 California Street, San Francisco
California 94104.

Editorial correspondence should be sent to the managing
Editor-in-Chief, Gordon G. Darkenwald, Graduate School
of Education, Rutgers University, 10 Seminary Place,
New Brunswick, New Jersey 08903.

Library of Congress Catalogue Card Number LC 83-82725
International Standard Serial Number ISSN 0195-2242
International Standard Book Number ISBN 87589-993-5

Cover art by Willi Baum
Manufactured in the United States of America

Ordering Information

The paperback sourcebooks listed below are published quarterly and can be ordered either by subscription or single-copy.

Subscriptions cost $35.00 per year for institutions, agencies, and libraries. Individuals can subscribe at the special rate of $25.00 per year *if payment is by personal check.* (Note that the full rate of $35.00 applies if payment is by institutional check, even if the subscription is designated for an individual.) Standing orders are accepted. Subscriptions normally begin with the first of the four sourcebooks in the current publication year of the series. When ordering, please indicate if you prefer your subscription to begin with the first issue of the *coming* year.

Single copies are available at $8.95 when payment accompanies order, and *all single-copy orders under $25.00 must include payment.* (California, New Jersey, New York, and Washington, D.C., residents please include appropriate sales tax.) For billed orders, cost per copy is $8.95 plus postage and handling. (Prices subject to change without notice.)

Bulk orders (ten or more copies) of any individual sourcebook are available at the following discounted prices: 10–49 copies, $8.05 each; 50–100 copies, $7.15 each; over 100 copies, *inquire.* Sales tax and postage and handling charges apply as for single copy orders.

To ensure correct and prompt delivery, all orders must give either the *name of an individual* or an *official purchase order number.* Please submit your order as follows:

Subscriptions: specify series and year subscription is to begin.
Single Copies: specify sourcebook code (such as, CE8) and first two words of title.

Mail orders for United States and Possessions, Latin America, Canada, Japan, Australia, and New Zealand to:
Jossey-Bass Inc., Publishers
433 California Street
San Francisco, California 94104

Mail orders for all other parts of the world to:
Jossey-Bass Limited
28 Banner Street
London EC1Y 8QE

New Directions for Continuing Education Series
Gordon G. Darkenwald, Alan B. Knox, *Editors-in-Chief*

CE1 *Enhancing Proficiencies of Continuing Educators,* Alan B. Knox
CE2 *Programming for Adults Facing Mid-Life Change,* Alan B. Knox
CE3 *Assessing the Impact of Continuing Education,* Alan B. Knox
CE4 *Attracting Able Instructors of Adults,* M. Alan Brown, Harlan G. Copeland
CE5 *Providing Continuing Education by Media and Technology,* Martin N. Chamberlain

CE6 *Teaching Adults Effectively,* Alan B. Knox
CE7 *Assessing Educational Needs of Adults,* Floyd C. Pennington
CE8 *Reaching Hard-to-Reach Adults,* Gordon G. Darkenwald, Gordon A. Larson
CE9 *Strengthening Internal Support for Continuing Education,* James C. Votruba
CE10 *Advising and Counseling Adult Learners,* Frank R. DiSilvestro
CE11 *Continuing Education for Community Leadership,* Harold W. Stubblefield
CE12 *Attracting External Funds for Continuing Education,* John Buskey
CE13 *Leadership Strategies for Meeting New Challenges,* Alan B. Knox
CE14 *Programs for Older Adults,* Morris A. Okun
CE15 *Linking Philosophy and Practice,* Sharan B. Merriam
CE16 *Creative Financing and Budgeting,* Travis Shipp
CE17 *Materials for Teaching Adults: Selection, Development, and Use,* John P. Wilson
CE18 *Strengthening Connections Between Education and Performance,* Stanley M. Grabowski
CE19 *Helping Adults Learn How to Learn,* Robert M. Smith
CE20 *Educational Outreach to Select Adult Populations,* Carol E. Kasworm
CE21 *Meeting the Educational Needs of Young Adults,* Gordon G. Darkenwald, Alan B. Knox
CE22 *Designing and Implementing Effective Workshops,* Thomas J. Sork

Contents

Editor's Notes   1
Hal Beder

Chapter 1. Interorganizational Cooperation: Why and How?   3
Hal Beder
Interorganizational cooperation is an effective strategy for gaining critical operating resources, and is based on the principle of reciprocal benefit.

Chapter 2. Collaboration in University Continuing Professional Education   23
Ronald M. Cervero
Through a continuing professional education program based on interorganizational cooperation, the University of Illinois at Chicago offers over 1500 separate programs per year.

Chapter 3. Who's in Control? A Case Study of University-Industry Collaboration   39
Arlene Fingeret
Substantial differences between the values and operating procedures of a university and a nuclear power utility destroy a promising collaborative effort.

Chapter 4. The Consequences of Mismanaged Interagency Collaborations   65
Thomas Valentine
A collaborative enterprise to provide adult career education dissolves in the wake of mismanaged interagency cooperation.

Chapter 5. Principles for Successful Collaboration   85
Hal Beder
Four themes characterize successful interorganizational collaboration efforts: reciprocity, system openness, an atmosphere of trust and commitment, and compatible organizational structures.

Index   91

Editor's Notes

The literature of education and social service is rife with what has become a contemporary dictum: cooperate. We are told that cooperation among organizations reduces competition, negates duplication of effort, and facilitates coordination of service delivery. Cooperation is a social good. Perhaps—but exhortations do not produce results, and organizations, when they do cooperate, seldom do so for altruistic reasons. In recognition of these facts, this volume approaches cooperation from the perspective of the benefits and costs that accrue to cooperating organizations. If we have been successful, the reader will come to understand the critical ingredients of establishing successful interorganizational cooperation and will become mindful of the costs that can be incurred so that these can be avoided.

In the first chapter, Beder provides the conceptual framework of the volume. Cervero, in the second chapter, provides a case study of the successful continuing professional education programs offered by the University of Illinois at Chicago. His conclusion: Interorganizational collaboration is a valuable tool for program development and success. Yet insight frequently derives as much from failure as from success. Accordingly, Fingeret in the third chapter analyzes an interorganizational collaboration that ultimately failed between a large university and a nuclear power company. The reasons for failure suggest problems to avoid in establishing cooperative relationships.

In the fourth chapter, Valentine continues this theme, providing us with a case analysis of the Crawford Adult Education Center, a program based on interorganizational collaboration that, although it began with great promise, never realized its potential. The lessons of Crawford Center powerfully demonstrate that failure to follow the principles of sound cooperation can result in disaster. In the final chapter, Beder summarizes and synthesizes the conclusions of the preceding three.

Hal Beder
Editor

Hal Beder is an associate professor of adult and continuing education, Graduate School of Education, Rutgers University, and directs the Rutgers' Center for Adult Development. He also serves as the editor of Adult Education Quarterly.

The basic principle of sound interorganizational cooperation is that an agency must give up something to get something.

Interorganizational Cooperation: Why and How?

Hal Beder

One of the problems in writing a chapter on developing continuing education programs though interorganizational cooperation is that continuing education agencies differ considerably. Hence, principles that apply to one agency do not necessarily apply to others. Given that problem, it seems reasonable to begin this chapter by characterizing the continuing education agencies from which material for this chapter has been derived and to which our discussion applies.

Characteristics of Continuing Education Agencies

Resource Insecurity. As organizations, continuing education agencies differ from elementary, secondary, and traditional undergraduate higher education organizations in several significant ways. We are all aware—and sometimes painfully—that continuing education units, in almost all cases, are attached to a parent organization for which continuing education is an ancillary function rather than the primary one. The implications are obvious to anyone who has worked in the field. Resources—"hard," dependable, secure resources—tend to be allocated to traditional functions, while adult continuing education generally has to pay its own way. When parent organization resources are constricted, as is frequently the case these days, continuing education is often the first to suffer cuts. As a result, not only are continuing education agencies constantly in search of resources needed to function, but, unlike other deans, directors, principals, or executives, continuing educators have inherited the responsibility for resource acquisition and must meet it if their programs are to prosper or even survive. Hence the first characteristic of the continuing education programs we write about here: chronic resource insecurity and the imperative of acquiring resources needed to operate.

Need for Flexibility. Traditional education in North America is more than a function, it is a national institution. A third grader in Clinton, New Jersey, is taught roughly the same things as a third grader in Racine, Wisconsin; a physics graduate of Rutgers University is prepared in the same way as a physics graduate of U.C.L.A. Research generates knowledge; curriculum developers organize it; publishers disseminate it; committees sanction it; instructors convey and assess the learning of it; learners learn it in preparation for things to come about which they know little. Class sessions are organized into terms, terms into years, years into degrees. This is not so with continuing education, for its goals and methods derive not from the educational system, but from the immediate needs of learners and organizations. Here too the implications are fairly obvious.

Terryberry (1968) and Emery and Trist (1965) have noted several types of organizational environments, ranging from the "placid environment" to the "turbulent field." A placid environment is relatively static. Not only is there little change, but individuals within the environment can identify the origin of the changes that effect them and can predict the consequences of those changes. Consider a nineteenth century rural New England town, for example.

In a turbulent field, however, the environment is dynamic, vibrant. Not only is change the norm, but the factors which cause it are far removed, generally unknown, and quite unpredictable. A Shah is deposed; an oil embargo imposed; a gasoline crisis generated; travel is curtailed; noncredit continuing education programs suffer correspondingly. The market for continuing education is thus affected by factors no continuing educator could have either predicted or controlled.

If we are to have learners and income, we must be flexible enough to meet learner and organizational needs in dynamic environments. We have to identify needs and markets as quickly as they develop. We must organize instruction, promote and conduct relevant programs, and then change direction as soon as those needs and markets transform into new ones. Thus, the second characteristic of the continuing education programs dealt with here is a need for great flexibility.

Autonomy. What happens when one component of an educational organization, the continuing education unit, must: (1) meet immediate learning needs, (2) be very flexible, and (3), acquire a large portion of its own resources, while the parent organization is (1) focused on preparatory learning or not even involved in education, (2) conservative, and (3) guaranteed sufficient resources to operate? The question is rhetorical; the answer, as McNeil (1980) points out, is organizational strain. As Beder (1979) notes, continuing education agencies must operate differently from their parent organizations if they are to be successful. To do so, and avoid organizational strain, they need a measure of autonomy from the parent sponsor. They have to be loosely coupled rather than tightly bound to the rules and structure of the parent entity. This is the third characteristic of the continuing education agencies dealt with here: need for operating autonomy.

Insecurity. To a certain extent, our last characteristic encompasses the others. Organizational insecurity is born in an environment where continuing education units must (1) continually justify themselves to parent organizations which are often more interested in other things, (2) acquire most of their own operating resources, and (3) serve a dynamic educational market. Continuing education agencies must successfully and continuously justify themselves to their sponsors and to the public. Our success is judged by the numbers and sometimes the quality of our programs, and perhaps unfortunately, by the income we produce. Our existence is not a constant, but a variable. If we fail to succeed we are relegated to the backwaters and to eventual extinction.

In summation, we view continuing education agencies as being chronically in need of operating resources and largely responsible for acquiring them themselves, oriented toward a dynamic educational market and hence in need of considerable flexibility, operating differently from their parent organizations and thus requiring operating autonomy, and, finally, faced with ongoing organizational insecurity. Although our characterization may sound bleak it is far from hopeless. There is a way to satisfy these difficult conditions. The solution is interagency cooperation and this is precisely what this chapter is about.

Why Cooperate?

In recent years the rhetoric of continuing education has been replete with exhortations to cooperate — as if cooperation were a virtue in itself, an axiomatic social good. This chapter takes a more pragmatic approach. Cooperation is important because through cooperation the adult education agency can achieve vital ends that it cannot achieve easily in other ways. But before we argue the case, an explanation of what we mean by cooperation is necessary. Cooperation is the process of working with other organizations and individuals to achieve mutual benefits. The important concept here is mutuality, for, as will be discussed at length later on, unless both parties benefit from a cooperative relationship, the relationship will be difficult to establish and short lived in duration.

Types of Cooperation

Although interagency cooperation takes many forms, there are four types of cooperation which are most prevalent. They are cosponsorship, referral, donor-receiver, and coordination.

Cosponsorship. In a cosponsorship the continuing education agency jointly offers a program with another agency.

Example. A continuing education agency has identified a need in the business community for training in the use of personal computers. To provide the training, the agency needs computers, relevant software and expert staff, none of which it possesses. The capital expense of purchasing the necessities is estimated at $110,000, a figure far beyond what the program can afford. To avoid the capital expense and yet still provide the training, a cosponsor relationship is established with a computer sales company which provides customer education to its clients. The computer company loans the hardware and software in anticipation of sales and provides expert instructors. Income above expenses is split between the continuing education agency and the computer company. An excellent program results; both parties benefit.

Referral. In a referral relationship other organizations and individuals refer learners to the continuing education agency. This is clearly important, for learners are our raw material without whom we can do nothing. Furthermore, in fee-financed programs there is a direct correspondence between numbers of learners and income.

Example. The Albany, New York, Adult Basic Education Program (ABE) had a referral relationship with the State Employment Service. The employment service was evaluated according to how many of its clients were placed in jobs. Yet many undereducated adults could not be placed due to lack of literacy skills and the employment service was constrained in fulfilling its mission. Similarly, the ABE program was evaluated according to the numbers of low literacy adults it educated. Yet recruitment of learners was a chronic problem; literacy as an end in itself attracted few people. Consequently, the employment service referred clients to the ABE program, where they were educated, became employable, and were referred back to the employment service. The ABE program gained learners, the employment service placed more clients, and learners obtained jobs they otherwise would not have had.

Donor-Receiver. In a donor-receiver relationship other organizations make outright donations to the continuing education agency for charitable or promotional purposes.

Example. The Continuing Education Center is a residential continuing education agency attached to a major university. It provides continuing education to various groups, most of which come from business and industry. The Philips Company is a high technology manufacturing company that produces word processors. It operates in a dynamic market which is highly competitive. Philips needed exposure for its products. Hence it donated a word processing system to the Continuing Education Center, which agreed to place the equipment in a prominent location where the business executive clients of the center could witness its use. The Philips Company gained a tax deduction and exposure for its product; the Continuing Education Center gained a word processing system.

Coordination. In a coordination relationship, continuing education agencies agree to coordinate activities so as to maximize efficiency, reduce harmful competition, and mutually assist each others' efforts.

Example. Most public providers include public schools, county colleges, county vocational schools, libraries, and the Cooperative Extension Service. Each provider needs public visibility, programming advice, and market information. Each also has the potential for offering programs which compete with those of the other providers. In response to the situation, county councils were organized by the State Education Department's Division of Adult Education. These councils meet monthly to coordinate activities, share ideas, and promote adult and continuing education in general. All parties benefit.

Cooperation as a Strategy for Success

As suggested previously, cooperation is a strategy that continuing education agencies can use productively to enhance the success of their programs. Before we explore this proposition in depth, however, it is important to explore what success means. Continuing education agencies exist within an organizational environment that contains the resources the agency needs to grow, prosper, and educate effectively. At the same time, however, the environment frequently poses constraints and threats which limit the agency in fulfilling its mission. To grossly oversimplify, a strategy for organizational success must include the means for acquiring resources while avoiding constraints.

In respect to this "open systems" success strategy, Yuchtman and Seashore (1967) note: "We propose accordingly to define the effectiveness of an organization in terms of its bargaining position, as reflected in the ability of the organization, in either absolute or relative terms, to exploit its environment in the acquisition of scarce and valued resources" (p. 481). From this perspective, organizational success for the continuing education agency depends on its ability to acquire needed resources from the environment and then to process them efficiently to create a quality educational product. As Beder (1978) notes, successful resource acquisition may result in a program development dynamic, as each increment of resources improves the agency's ability to gain still more needed resources.

Example. The Jointure for Community Adult Education of Central New Jersey conducted a fledgling English-as-a-second-language (ESL) program as part of its adult literacy effort. Initially ESL was staffed with part-time teachers and served approximately fifty students. Aspiring to develop the ESL program into something more substantial, the director realized that he would need more funds and more expertise. Consequently, he formed a cooperative relationship with a local university adult and continuing education graduate program. As part of their coursework, graduate students conducted a needs assessment and wrote a funding proposal for an experimental, community-based ESL effort. The prestige of the university and the technical expertise in planning and grantsmanship of the graduate students abetted successful funding of the project. The grant funds thus acquired permitted employment of a full-time project director who devoted part of her talents to promotion. The result was greater community visibility and an increase in students.

At a countywide meeting of adult educators, the director learned that Comprehensive Education and Training Act (CETA) funds were available for ESL instruction. When the grant funding terminated, he then proposed to CETA that the program, which had earned a reputation for quality, be continued on CETA support. CETA funding was secured and more staff were hired, enabling total reorganization of the ESL program and resulting in even greater numbers of students. Thus, as each new resource was secured from the environment at large, the continuing education agency found it easier to secure additional resources. The ESL component grew from a program serving fifty learners with an $8,000 budget to a program serving 200 learners with a budget of $118,622.

Our preliminary discussion of strategy leads to the following principles: (1) The primary objectives of a continuing education agency are to acquire needed and valuable resources and then to convert them into a quality educational product that appeals to learners, (2) the first step in meeting these objectives is to identify what resources are most needed, and (3) there are essentially three ways in which needed resources, once identified, may be obtained: competition, cooptation, and cooperation. Each strategy requires interorganizational interaction.

Competition is generally a poor strategy because it breeds antagonists who, although they may lose today, may prevail tomorrow. Cooptation, turning your antagonists into supporters, can be very valuable but does not generally lead to resource acquisition. Cooperation is the antithesis of competition and almost always promotes resource acquisition. Hence, cooperation is generally the most productive strategy for agency success. Through cooperation, continuing education agencies can obtain valuable and vital resources while neutralizing antagonists and promoting support among their important publics.

The Essential Resources for Survival

There are several resources which all continuing education agencies must obtain. They are: money, learners, staff, information, domain, and power.

Money. Money is a particularly valuable resource because it can be used to purchase other resources. It can be obtained in two basic ways. Either it can be given, as when it is allocated from a hard budget, or it can be earned. Increasingly, the first option is denied to continuing education amid cries of "you shall be self-supporting." If money is to be earned, something must be offered to the public for which the public is willing to pay. Cooperation can assist.

Example. A large state university's continuing medical education (CME) program is operated on a self-supporting basis. Each year the medical school advances to the CME program a line of credit which is used as capital in mounting programs for physicians. At the end of the fiscal year, the account must be balanced. Deficits must be absorbed in staff reductions, which restrict adequate functioning.

Several programs were planned for a fall term, including a large income-producing conference during the first week of December. This conference, for ophthalmologists, entailed substantial fixed costs for promotion and materials development. Unfortunately and unexpectedly, for the first time in seventy-five years it snowed; the conference failed, the program found itself $10,000 in deficit, and with six months left in the fiscal year prospects for a balanced account were bleak.

Seeking to recoup losses, the dean of continuing education contacted several prominent pharmaceutical companies that sold products to physicians and depended on doctors' prescriptions for their corporate incomes. One company agreed to fully underwrite a program on new advances in steroids. Since all costs were covered, the fees collected were pure income to be applied against the deficit. Another company agreed to pay for the publication costs of the materials developed for the failed ophthalmology conference. The materials were published, and sold to ophthalmologists. Again the income was applied to the deficit. A third company made an outright grant to the continuing education program. At the end of the fiscal year, the continuing education program showed a $5,000 surplus. The pharmaceutical companies benefitted from the tax-deductible promotion of their products. The continuing education program accomplished educational and financial objectives.

Learners. As noted above, learners comprise our raw material. Without them there can be no continuing education. Furthermore, when fees are paid, money resources increase. Not only can cooperation help acquire learners, but it can help continuing education programs recruit those learners whom they especially desire to serve.

Example. The Institute for Educational Development is the continuing professional education agency of a graduate school of education. It is a new program and had been experiencing problems in identifying a market for its programs. Although public school teachers and administrators were an obvious option, school districts showed declining enrollments and severe budget problems. Teachers' salaries were low and had remained constant during a period of years characterized by severe inflation. Hence, public school personnel were demoralized and reluctant to pay fees for staff development activities. Therefore, the Institute had great difficulty in recruiting them. Realizing that it would have to identify new markets for a source of learners, the Institute approached a large multinational corporation well known for the size and quality of its training department. Conversations with corporate training personnel resulted in acknowledgement of a problem: Although the training department was highly successful in providing training to the company's employees, it could not convince top management to mount a staff development program for its own trainers. Trainers had to learn their skills on the job. This took time and limited trainer productivity and effectiveness. Moreover, the company was degree-conscious and considered advanced degrees in promotion decisions.

Seeing the possibilities, the institute contacted the continuing education faculty for assistance. Faculty, corporation trainers, and institute staff then jointly planned a graduate degree concentration focusing on training in business and industry. Three courses were developed addressing the training model, materials design, and platform skills. The courses were then taught in the company's sophisticated training facility on both a credit and noncredit basis. Both university graduate students and corporate training personnel attended.

The benefits are clear. The institute and the adult education graduate program gained access to a new source of learners—learners who were willing to participate and had the means to pay fees. The company benefitted from the ability to provide staff development to its trainers at a cost far below that of other options.

Staff. Clearly, no organization can function without staff to do its work. Not only must a continuing education agency have staff, it must have staff with the required expertise. This is particularly a problem for continuing education agencies with part-time "adjunct" teaching staffs. How do such agencies acquire instructors with competencies in specialized subject matter? Cooperation can be a useful strategy.

Example. The Institute for Municipal Training is a university-based continuing education agency established to train municipal employees such as tax assessors and building inspectors. The full-time staff of the institute are professional continuing educators. Subject matter expertise is the purview of part-time instructors. To acquire competent staff, the institute cooperates closely with professional associations representing municipal employee specialties, for example, tax assessors. The president of each association is asked to appoint an education committee comprised of eminent specialists in the field. The committee then works closely with institute staff to develop curriculum, materials, and specific programs. Members of the committee then become a pool of instructors who are hired to teach the courses developed.

Information. Although information is important to any organization, it is particularly important to educational agencies that must perform in a dynamic market. Continuing education agencies must have sources of information regarding learner needs and preferences, competition, and the success or failure of their programs. Without such information the agency cannot determine what to offer, to whom, where, when, and how. Information must be accurate and timely and the flow of information must be continuous and consistent.

Information flows from a source through a channel to a receiver. Partners in cooperation make excellent sources. Links between organizations make very good channels for several reasons:

1. Cooperative relationships are generally characterized by a high degree of trust and respect. Thus, information received from partners in cooperative ventures is generally trustworthy.

2. Maintenance of cooperative relationships generally entails frequent communication, and information valuable to the continuing education agency is often conveyed informally during the course of other business. Hence, cooperative relationships are a good source of constant and continuous information that is readily accessible.

3. As will be discussed at length later in this chapter, continuing education agencies tend to cooperate with organizations that complement rather than duplicate what the continuing education agency does. As a result, an agency's network of cooperating partners generally contains information which, although relevant to continuing education, comes from sources outside the continuing education community. Hence networks of cooperating organizations vastly increase the scope and diversity of information available to the continuing education agency.

Domain. Domain refers to the sphere of influence in which an organization is legitimately empowered to operate. The concept is nearly synonymous with the more colloquial term *turf.* Religious adult education programs can offer Bible classes but not continuing legal education, for example, and although community colleges can offer continuing education for undergraduate credit, only four-year colleges and universities can offer graduate credit. Domain is obviously an important concept because the wider an agency's domain, the more options it has for programming and the larger the market it can potentially serve. Most community colleges, for example, can offer virtually anything they wish while hospitals must focus on health-related offerings. However, when the domains of two continuing education agencies overlap, or when one agency tries to expand its domain and in doing so encroaches on the domain of another, the potential for conflict is high and what is popularly known as a turf fight can result. Domain conflicts are almost always destructive, for they sap energy that should be directed toward other activities and they create enemies. Fortunately, cooperation is an excellent strategy for extending domain without eliciting conflict. Cosponsorship represents such a strategy.

Example. The Institute for Research on Adult Education (IRAE) is a semi-autonomous research institute reporting to the provost of a major university. Although the institute is authorized to offer continuing education on a self-supporting basis, most of its continuing education efforts had been esoteric and directed toward a small but supportive group of researchers. Most of IRAE's energies had been directed toward conducting sponsored research and performing needs assessments and evaluations for other continuing education agencies. In conducting a needs assessment for the physical education department, IRAE staff learned that alcohol and drug abuse among athletes was a major issue. The physical education department, however, had neither the interest nor capacity to address the problem.

Recognizing the potential for a high visibility and important continuing education program, IRAE staff considered developing a series of nationally marketed seminars for athletes and coaches on sports and substance abuse. Income from the series might supplement the meager research budget upon which IRAE depended and might also be used to support professional travel.

There was a problem however—a significant one: Alcohol abuse was the domain of the University's Institute of Alcohol Studies, and the medical aspects of substance abuse were the preserve of the medical school's Department of Sports Medicine. To offer the program threatened to trigger a major turf fight which IRAE was convinced it would lose.

The solution was relatively simple. IRAE staff contacted the Institute of Alcohol Studies and the medical school's Continuing Medical Education Department and a three-way cosponsorship was established. IRAE and the Continuing Medical Education Department jointly planned and organized the program, while the Institute of Alcohol Studies supplied instructors, who were paid. The net income from the program, which was very successful, was divided between the planner-organizers and was subsequently used by IRAE to expand significantly its research activities.

Power. Power, defined as the ability to induce persons and other agencies to do what they normally would not do, is a very important resource. Although power is important for any organization, it is particularly crucial for continuing education agencies for at least two reasons. First, as noted earlier, continuing education agencies are almost always attached to sponsoring organizations for which continuing education is a support or ancillary function. Continuing education has been characterized as marginal (Clark, 1958) and on the periphery

(Moses, 1971). Frequently policies enacted by the sponsor as necessary for governing the primary function are injurious to continuing education. Regulations governing course credit, for example, frequently limit college and university continuing education programs, and regulations concerning school building usage plague public school programs. Similarly, union contract provisions regarding overtime often cause problems for industrial trainers. Clearly, it is important for continuing education to influence such policies, but all too frequently continuing education operates from a low power position by virtue of the fact that it is considered to be peripheral rather than central to the sponsor organization. Secondly, just as the continuing education agency needs power to influence internal policies, it also needs power to influence the external environment. When other organizations threaten continuing education's domain, such threats must be countered. When regulatory agencies propose rules injurious to continuing education, those rules must be blocked or modified.

Cooperation is a very effective strategy for acquiring power, as influential cooperating partners can serve as important allies in applying power. This is particularly important in internal conflicts, for frequently continuing educators find it difficult to resist harmful policies of their sponsors because, as employees of the sponsor, they are part of the chain of command. However, external allies are removed from the chain of command and can influence upper echelons of the sponsor. This makes it possible for continuing educators to exert influence without having to confront their superiors.

Example. The Goat's Bay Continuing Education Program is attached to a highly politicized urban school district. Goat's Bay offers diverse programs to the general public, including adult literacy, vocational, and avocational subjects. The program is primarily self-supporting and derived a large portion of its income from a popular and long-running concert series. Income from concerts was used to subsidize other important, but less cost-effective, programs. Maintaining the concert series required application of a major principle: never cancel. Goat's Bay is an unsafe neighborhood; residents traveled at risk to the evening concerts. To arrive and find a concert cancelled caused understandable resentment. The director realized that if residents ever lost faith in the program's ability to deliver, the concert series—and a major income source—was doomed.

It was the morning before the most important concert of the series. A famous and very popular opera star was to sing. The house was sold out, and the phones had been ringing for days with inquiries about the availability of standing room. At 9:00 A.M. the director received a phone call from the opera company. The company's lead role singer for the evening was sick; he could not sing; the concert series' star would have to fill in; there could be no concert at Goat's Bay that night. "But," reminded the director, "we have a contract." The phone call ended with no resolution of the crisis. At 9:30 A.M. another call was received. It was the chancellor of the entire school system. The message was short and direct. The contract would not be enforced. The opera star would sing, but at the opera house, not at Goat's Bay. The director of continuing education was faced with a dilemma. He did not wish to confront his loftiest superior, but, at the same time, a cancellation would be disastrous to his program.

Fortunately, there were diplomatic channels. The director of the Goat's Bay program had established an advisory panel consisting of influential supporters from the community and from the organizations with which he cooperated. One of the members was a skilled and influential lawyer. The director called the lawyer, explained the situation, and by 3:00 P.M. an injunction had been issued enjoining the opera star from singing at the opera that night. Bear in mind that this action was initiated by an "interested member of the community" rather than by an official of the program. Negotiations between the opera and the Goat's Bay program were underway by 3:30 P.M. and a solution was agreed upon. Although the opera star was to sing at the opera that night, he would perform two future concerts at Goat's Bay for the price of one. Although community residents had to endure a postponement, the two-for-one provision satisfied them and the concert program retained its credibility.

We have characterized continuing education agencies as being organizationally insecure and in chronic need of flexibility, autonomy, and resources. We have argued that cooperation is an excellent strategy for overcoming these problems. External sources of money certainly promote autonomy; money and power combat organizational insecurity. Large numbers of students reduce insecurity and help create income. Cooperation can help an agency attain these resources. However, cooperation entails its own costs, as well as posing the problem of how to establish and maintain cooperative relationships.

The Guiding Principle

Establishing cooperative relationships involves a basic principle which should be remembered even if everything else in this chapter is forgotten. It is the principle of *reciprocity*. The basis for establishing cooperative relationships is mutual, reciprocal benefit. If both parties to a cooperative relationship benefit, the relationship will be easy to develop and will remain healthy over time. If one or both parties fail to benefit, the relationship will crumble. Solid cooperation results when each party benefits by giving up something valued less than that which it gains.

If reciprocal benefit is the primary basis for cooperation, the issue becomes one of finding suitable cooperating partners who stand to gain from the relationship. The key is to look for organizations with goals that complement continuing education, rather than organizations similar to the continuing education agency. The reason for this is simple: Similar organizations generally need the same resources as continuing education and are therefore not in a position to trade, while complementary organizations need different things—things continuing education may possess. Hence, it is easier to bargain.

Example One. A large urban hospital employed numerous housekeeping and maintenance workers who, despite the fact that they spoke English poorly, worked in close proximity to patients. Doctors and nurses became concerned when there were several incidents jeopardizing patient safety. Apparently the employees who spoke English poorly could not read warning signs and could not understand directions given by the nursing staff. Rules and procedures regarding sterility and moving patients were being ignored. There were two logical solutions: fire the workers or educate them. No one wanted to fire otherwise competent employees, but the hospital had neither the expertise nor the funds for education.

At the same time the city's adult literacy program was experiencing difficulty recruiting and retaining students and its funding source was threatening to reduce its allocation for lack of sufficient enrollment. The hospital needed ESL instruction, the adult literacy program needed students—a perfect situation for cosponsorship. The hospital administrator contacted the director of the adult literacy program and a cosponsorship was established. The literacy program supplied a teacher in return for a substantial and stable supply of students. The hospital supplied space and paid the workers for the hours they spent in class. The needs of the hospital for English-speaking staff complemented the need of the adult literacy program for participants.

Example Two. Central County College is a community college in a relatively affluent section of New Jersey which had traditionally concentrated on preparing liberal arts students for transfer to four-year institutions. As the county grew, however, there was more and more demand for adult vocational programs. After a comprehensive needs analysis, the college administration decided that its initial efforts at curriculum expansion should be directed toward preparing laboratory technicians, for not only were the area hospitals in chronic short supply of laboratory technicians, but there was a large concentration of pharmaceutical companies in the vicinity which could employ graduates. The problems, however, were substantial. Where was the college to get qualified faculty and where were they to acquire the sophisticated and expensive equipment for students to train on?

Crestview, Eastside, and Saint Marks were the three major hospitals in the county. None had an adequate supply of laboratory staff and there were constant complaints from doctors and nurses that laboratory tests were taking too long and were occasionally inaccurate. Central County College's dean contacted each hospital with a proposition: Accept our students on an internship basis and teach them how to use sophisticated equipment and techniques; in return they can perform routine laboratory tasks for you. The proposition was accepted, the internship established. The hospitals thereby received a source of semi-professional labor, which freed their professional staff from routine work, and Central County College received expertise and access to sophisticated equipment.

Practical Tips

If the reciprocity principle is followed and if organizations that have needs which complement continuing education are sought for cooperation, the continuing education agency will be well on its way to establishing productive cooperative relationships. There are, however, several principles which—if followed—will facilitate success. They are:

1. *Start with the contacts you already have,* for example, your personal network of friends and colleagues, or the organizations with which your agency already does business in a noneducational capacity. In most cases, you will already have established a trust relationship with these contacts and you will have firsthand knowledge of their needs and operations. For example, the former director of adult education in an upstate New York city had as a contact his own mother, an official of the State Employment Service. From her he learned that poorly-educated clients could not be placed in jobs, a situation which concerned the employment service. The director contacted the employment service, and, aided by his mother, established a referral relationship, which over the years resulted in many hundreds of learners for the adult literacy program.

2. *Always support your cooperation partners in public;* save criticism

for private encounters. Support engenders support and public criticism breeds mistrust.

Example. An adult literacy program had established a productive referral relationship with the Neighborhood Youth Corps. On occasion, however, youthful students were unruly, a problem which, though solvable, was troublesome. However, program staff began to complain in public. The Neighborhood Youth Corps was offended and the referral was terminated. When the director learned the reason for termination, staff were quietly admonished and the principle "never bad-mouth our partners" was established as a basic rule of the agency.

3. *Remember that relationships established today can pay off with considerable "interest" in the future.* Competent contacts tend to rise in the system, gaining in power and influence, thus being in an even better position to help the continuing education agency. For example, a public school continuing education program had established a cooperative relationship with a government agency. The department head with which the continuing education director worked became the commissioner of the agency five years later. The informal relationship developed between the two individuals later became a link to power for the continuing education program.

4. *Maximize your time.* Many productive cooperative relationships are established as an outgrowth of normal day-to-day interaction. Never miss a chance to negotiate informally at professional association, coordinating council, service club and other meetings. But do not waste your time seeking cooperation with organizations with which there is little hope of reciprocity.

Hidden Costs of Cooperation

Although the benefits of cooperation can be very substantial, it is important to realize that cooperation can also entail significant costs in dislocation, goal displacement, and loss of control.

Time. Establishing cooperation takes time that could be spent on other vital activities. Generally speaking, newer agencies must devote considerably more time to developing cooperative relationships. This is so because newer agencies have less visibility and less well-established reputations. Thus they have to actively seek and initiate contacts. As the agency grows, however, it becomes more visible and its reputation becomes established. Once this happens, other organizations begin to seek it as a cooperating partner and the time spent on seeking and initiating is greatly reduced. The effort then shifts to maintaining, rather than establishing, cooperative relationships, and maintenance generally requires less of a time commitment.

Dislocation. Occasionally, cooperative relationships turn out to be incompatible with the operations of the continuing education agency, or the partner, or both, and this causes organizational dislocation, internal strain, and ultimately, termination of the relationship.

Example. A health clinic located in a government housing project noted that many of its practical nursing staff lacked sufficient education to continue for registered nurse training and in some cases could not perform their jobs adequately for lack of literacy skills. A cosponsorship was established with the local adult literacy program, which provided instruction during working hours. However, when nurses left the ward to participate, other nurses were required to "cover." Coffee breaks for covering nurses had to be eliminated and the workers complained bitterly. Then the housekeeping and clerical staff learned of the literacy program and requested permission to participate. The clinic, however, could not afford the personnel benefit of released time for these workers, and there were more complaints. Eventually the program was abandoned.

Goal Displacement. If a continuing education agency is not careful, it can establish cooperative relationships which deter it from fulfilling its mission. Although the short-term benefits may be great enough to make such relationships attractive, the long-term ramifications can be injurious indeed.

Example. A New England antipoverty agency conducted continuing education activities designed to promote the social mobility of poor people. Among these activities was a state-funded English-as-a-second-language program. Recruitment for the ESL program had been difficult, however. Coupled with a high drop-out rate, enrollment had been a chronic problem. At the same time, a local hospital had been having problems with its foreign interns and residents. Poor English-speaking ability made it difficult for these doctors to communicate, and their orders sometimes went unheeded. The hospital asked the continuing education agency to supply ESL instruction, and the continuing education agency agreed because it needed an adequate supply of committed learners. It did so despite the fact that the foreign doctors and interns were hardly poor. Although the continuing education agency did benefit in the short-run by increasing enrollments, it was eventually criticized severely by the community and by its funding source for abrogating its commitment to the poor. In the long run, the loss in credibility and reputation far outweighed the gain in enrollment.

Control. As mentioned earlier, in each cooperative relationship the continuing education agency must relinquish something in exchange for what it receives. In many cases, the continuing education agency must relinquish a measure of control. Two issues can engender diminution of control. First, in order to satisfy its cooperating partner, the continuing education agency must often abide by the rules, procedures, and decision making system of its cooperating partners. For example, the continuing education program sponsored by a graduate school of business administration was interested in expanding its offerings into the area of real estate, but had little experience in this field and had neither visibility nor reputation among real estate agents. To promote success of its incipient real estate offerings, the continuing education agency decided to cosponsor courses with the state realtors' association, which agreed as its part of the bargain to sanction the courses, to promote them, to provide sites, and to suggest instructors. Although several successful courses were conducted, the relationship soon ran into trouble. The Realtors' Association constitution required that every decision requiring expenditure of funds be sanctioned by the governing board. Decision making at the board level, however, was highly political and outcomes were difficult to predict. Policies affecting the cosponsorship, and hence the continuing education agency, were constantly changing and the result was a total lack of control. In such an atmosphere of uncertainty, effective programming was impossible and the relationship was terminated.

The second issue regarding control can result in the most severe cost of all—resource dependency. We have constantly harped on the point that cooperation is an effective strategy in resource acquisition. However, when a continuing education agency receives all or a critical amount of its vital resources from one cooperator, it can become dependent on that partner. If the dependent continuing education agency loses its benefactor organization, resource starvation can result. Likewise, organizations upon which the continuing agency are highly dependent are in the powerful position of being able to dictate policy to the continuing education agency. For example, in the early 1970s a public school adult education program in New York State established a highly successful cosponsorship with the Welfare Incentive Program (WIN). WIN referred large numbers of learners to the adult education program and paid them a stipend for attending. Hence the adult education program was never concerned with a sufficient supply of learners, and, in fact, grew considerably. Eventually WIN students accounted for 90 percent of the learners. Then disaster struck. WIN was restructured— no more stipends for adult literacy. Ninety percent of the program's students left within two weeks. One of the largest programs in the state was reduced to a skeleton.

A basic and vital principle to follow in establishing cooperative relationships is to avoid substantial resource dependency. There is a simple test to ascertain vulnerability: List each organization which is a major supplier of vital resources to your continuing education agency along with the resource it supplies. Then ask yourself of each, could we survive without this one? If the answer is no, the continuing education agency is vulnerable and needs to diversify its source of that resource supply by developing cooperative relationships with other organizations capable of supplying it.

Summary

Cooperation has been extolled for many and diverse reasons. Cooperation reduces duplication of effort, sometimes diminishes pernicious competition, can promote efficiency, and allows for mutual efforts at solving social problems. Yet rather than discussing cooperation as a social good, we have focused on cooperation as a major agency development strategy.

Through cooperation with other agencies, continuing education programs can secure vital resources such as money, learners, staff, information, extended domain, and power. The key to success is the principle of reciprocal benefit: Each cooperating partner offers resources valued less in exchange for resources valued more. Hence both partners benefit, and because they benefit the relationship is productive and healthy.

Yet despite the benefits to cooperation, there are costs to avoid. Establishing cooperative relationships takes time, especially for newer continuing education programs which lack public visibility. It can produce organizational dislocation and result in a displacement of organizational goals. Furthermore, in nearly every cooperative relationship both parties must relinquish a measure of control. This becomes a serious problem when a continuing education agency becomes overly dependent for resources on a small number of cooperating partners which it cannot afford to lose.

References

Beder, H. W. "An Environmental Interaction Model for Agency Development in Adult Education." *Adult Education,* 1978, *28* (3), 176-190.

Beder, H. W. "The Relationship of Community and Sponsor System Support to Selected Aspects of Adult Education Agency Functioning." *Adult Education,* 1979, *29* (2), 96-107.

Clark, B. *Adult Education in Transition: A Study of Institutional Insecurity.* Berkeley: University of California Press, 1958.

Emery, R. E., and Trist, E. L. "The Causal Texture of Organizational Environments." *Human Relations,* 1965, *18* (1), 21–32.

McNeil, P. *Community College Adult Education Growth: A Theoretical Analysis Using Grounded Theory Methodology.* Unpublished doctoral dissertation, Rutgers University, 1980.

Moses, S. *The Learning Force: A More Comprehensive Framework for Educational Policy.* Syracuse, N.Y.: Publications in Continuing Education, 1971.

Terryberry, S. "The Evolution of Organizational Environments." *Administrative Science Quarterly,* 1968, *12* (4), 590–613.

Yuchtman, E., and Seashore, S. "A System Resource Approach to Organizational Effectiveness." *American Sociological Review,* 1967, *32* (6), 891–903.

Hal Beder is an associate professor of adult and continuing education, Graduate School of Education, Rutgers University, and directs the Rutgers' Center for Adult Development. He also serves as the editor of Adult Education Quarterly. *The assistance of Gordon Darkenwald and Doreen Hackley in preparing this chapter is gratefully acknowledged.*

At the University of Illinois at Chicago, collaboration is the primary strategy for developing continuing professional education programs in the health care arena.

Collaboration in University Continuing Professional Education

Ronald M. Cervero

There is little doubt that interorganizational collaboration is emerging as one of the major issues in continuing professional education (CPE). A recently published book, *Power and Conflict in Continuing Professional Education* (Stern, 1983), is entirely devoted to the issues relevant to the organization and provision of CPE. One of its central themes is the need for more collaboration among providers. At present, however, the provision of CPE in most professions is characterized by organizations offering CPE with little regard for what other providers are doing. It is not surprising, then, that the two issues addressed most often are "Who should provide what?" and "Should providers be encouraged to compete or collaborate?"

Houle (1980) has identified seven dominant types of providers: autonomous groups (for example, journal clubs, teacher centers), professional associations, professional schools, the non-professional school sectors of universities, places of employment, independent providers of learning opportunities (for example, entrepreneurs), and purveyors of professional supplies and equipment. Each is described as having distinctive strengths as a provider of CPE. The most powerful and pervasive providers are the professional associations, universities and professional schools, and employers. Independent providers are seen by some as a fourth major provider (Suleiman, 1983).

Most of the literature on competition versus collaboration in CPE concludes that while collaboration is to be preferred, competition is more prevalent. This may be a function of the competitive spirit of American enterprise which Houle (1980, p. 194) sums up as follows: "Let the various providers do what seems best and the test of the marketplace will prevail."

Hohmann (1980), as well as other writers, has described the advantages and disadvantages of collaboration in CPE. Among the advantages are better coordination of offerings, closer links between preservice education and continuing education, and higher quality program production from shared resources. Disadvantages include lengthened time spent in program planning and implementation, which may lead to outdated offerings, and dominance by one provider over the others.

Most of the previously cited literature that concludes that competition is much more common than collaboration is not data based. The small amount of literature on this topic that is data based shows a strikingly different picture. Knox (1982) conducted a comprehensive study by analyzing university-based CPE efforts in five fields—medicine, pharmacy, social work, education, and law. He found that while small programs seemed unconcerned about working with other providers, "The directors of the large offices depended on effective relationships with other providers to maintain the size and diversity of their effort. They did so by cosponsoring activities that would have had less attendance if provided independently" (p. 122).

A national study of association-university collaboration determined that 48 percent of associations and 85 percent of universities had undertaken collaborative programming (Nowlen and Stern, 1981). Similarly, a national study of all accredited medical schools in the United States found that approximately 70 percent cosponsor ongoing continuing medical education programs with community hospitals (Younghouse, 1983). Among the consequences of these collaborative arrangements for the medical schools, as reported by the deans, were that they: (1) fulfilled part of the medical school's mission and goals, (2) enhanced the medical school's image and visibility, (3) provided visibility to new medical school faculty, and (4) increased referrals to the medical school's teaching hospitals or clinics.

In addition to these comprehensive studies of collaboration, there are many descriptions of actual collaborative programs. Several examples come from the fields of teaching (Davies and Aquino, 1975) and medicine (Manning and others, 1979). The empirical literature, as well as the anecdotal, leads to the conclusion that interorganizational collaboration is extensively practiced by CPE programs.

A weakness of the literature cited thus far is the lack of a theoretical framework for understanding and explaining various manifestations of interorganizational collaboration. This primarily descriptive literature suggests that collaborative arrangements are fairly common and beneficial. However, a theoretical framework would be valuable in constructing conceptual tools for the practice of CPE.

Beder has developed such a framework for interorganizational collaboration in continuing education. (Beder and Smith, 1977; Beder, 1978). The first study was empirical and concluded that the success of adult basic education programs was largely due to "the effective establishment and maintenance of comprehensive interorganizational relationships or 'linkages'" (Beder and Smith, 1977, p. 1). His second study was a theoretical paper that argued that the success of a continuing education agency depends on its ability to secure resources from its environment, such as participants, money, information, power, and domain. These resources may be obtained through strategically planned interorganizational linkages. Beder then proposed a number of internal organizational and environmental characteristics that are conducive to the development of linkages.

A Case Study in a Theoretical Framework

In order to describe interorganizational collaboration within the context of a theoretical framework, a case study of a university-based CPE agency is presented here. The agency studied is the continuing education unit of the University of Illinois at Chicago (UIC). The agency was selected because it is responsible for total campus continuing professional education programming, and because it is a large, comprehensive unit with many interorganizational ties. Specifically, the study examined the unit's response to the six health-related professional schools and colleges, and to large, comprehensive programs emanating from the professional schools of engineering, architecture, and the college of liberal arts and sciences.

The UIC case study is based on a total of six hours of audiotaped interviews completed on two separate days with the director of Continuing Education and Public Service, and on personal interaction with UIC since 1979. The purpose of this case study is to describe the director's perceptions, and his actions, and to reflect upon UIC activities that are demonstrative of interorganizational collaboration.

Four basic questions will be addressed through the framework presented by Beder in Chapter One:
1. What resources does the agency seek from the environment?
2. What types of cooperative relationships does the agency form with its environment to obtain these resources?
3. What factors help explain the extent to which the agency has formed cooperative relationships?
4. What are the benefits and costs of these relationships to the agency?

Description of the Agency

The state of Illinois, in general, and the metropolitan Chicago area, specifically, constitute the environment of UIC. Chicago's West Side is home to about forty health care institutions, including two medical schools (one housed at the University of Illinois at Chicago). This area comprises one of the greatest densities of health care institutions anywhere. Within the Chicago area are located five additional medical schools. There are numerous state and national professional associations, such as the American Medical Association, American Dental Association, American Hospital Association, and the Joint Commission on Accreditation of Hospitals, located in Chicago.

The University of Illinois is the state's land-grant institution and its largest university. Until 1982, there were three separate campuses: one at Urbana-Champaign, one at the West Side Medical Center, and one at Chicago Circle. The last two are both located in Chicago and, in 1982, were combined into one administrative unit, the University of Illinois at Chicago. The subject of the case study, the CPE administrative unit, is housed at the West Side Medical Center. There are additional continuing education units at the other two campuses. The medical center complex is one of the largest health science centers in the world. The university's preservice professional training programs have many formal affiliations with other institutions in the Chicago area. For example, medicine has fifty-two affiliations, nursing has twenty, and allied health has about fifteen.

There are fifty staff members at the medical center assigned to the CPE function. Twenty are directly responsible to the director and are located at the Chicago campus, the Rockford School of Medicine, the Peoria School of Medicine, and the School of Clinical Medicine at Urbana. These last three locations are the university's clinical training campuses. The other thirty staff members represent assistant and associate deans plus their staffs in each of six colleges: associated health professions, dentistry, medicine, nursing, pharmacy, and public health. The UIC staff at each location develop programs for all six professional groups in cooperation with the CPE staff of each college. The continuing education programs of medicine and pharmacy are nationally accredited by their respective professional associations. The program's budget is in excess of one million dollars.

In fiscal year 1980, 1,585 separate programs, ranging from one-hour events to conferences of several days duration, were offered. The director estimates that 70 percent of these programs were cosponsored by external agencies. The number of programs and participants has stayed relatively stable over the last five years, with a total of 40,000 participants having been served in that time.

Tangible Resources

To a large extent, the success of a continuing education agency rests on its ability to obtain resources from its environment. Thus the acquisition and maintenance of an adequate supply of resources becomes the operational definition of the purposes of the agency once it has reached an advanced stage of development (Benson, 1975). These resources can be described as tangible (participants, money, information, and facilities) and intangible (power, prestige, domain). All are sought by UIC, although some resources are more highly valued than others.

Participants are the primary tangible resource sought. While the reasons for this may be obvious, they are nonetheless worth stating. The agency's mission of providing health professions with continuing education could not be accomplished without participants. This resource is also important because it is translated into money; about two-thirds of UIC's funding is derived from participant fees.

Money is an important resource, but it is not as essential as participants. In the view of the director, funds "are not what make CPE go." Quality programs, rather than money, produce participants. Money from sources other than participants' fees, such as grants or gifts, accounts for about 10 percent of the agency's budget. A pharmaceutical company, for example, may cover the expenses for a program that pertains to one of its new drugs.

In the UIC context, information is a highly valued resource, because it increases the likelihood of acquiring participants. Information regarding potential participants' interests, wants, and needs (in terms of content, desired locations, and price) is valuable to the extent that it can be used to develop programs that produce participants. An example was given by the director. The Illinois Department of Registration and Education had suspended the licenses of a group of physicians and was requiring them to participate in an education program to address their problems before renewing their licenses. UIC received this information (a form of needs assessment), and developed a program that produced two tangible resources, participants and money. Thus, information is an enabling resource used to acquire the most important resource, participants.

Facilities are another important enabling resource. Although UIC has its own conference facilities, 70 percent of its programs are held at a cosponsoring agency's facility. The prime value of cosponsor's facilities is their proximity to the participants' workplace, and, in fact, most programs are held at the learners' workplace. For example, UIC cosponsors a weekly series of "grand rounds" in primary care medicine with several community hospitals.

Tangible resources are the raw materials without which the UIC continuing education unit could not operate. These resources are generally garnered through open negotiation with other institutions in the environment. Yet tangible resources are transitory: Participants enter and leave the system at will; information is useful only as it pertains to specific programs; profits from continuing education are generally used to support new and innovative projects within the institution. Their importance is gauged by the extent to which they increase the agency's intangible resources—power, prestige, and domain.

Intangible Resources

Power, prestige, and domain, on the other hand, are lasting resources, once obtained, and further UIC's overall position among its competitors. While intangible resources are actively sought from the environment, they are, generally, not discussed openly. In negotiating with a community hospital, UIC might seek information about learning needs and an attractive facility. Yet the long-term benefit to UIC is its legitimacy as a provider of CPE in the eyes of that community hospital. Legitimacy gives UIC regular access to information, facilities, participants, and money. It is not surprising, then, that one of the director's main goals is that "every health professional in Illinois would look toward the University of Illinois as the most legitimate provider of CPE." To the extent that this goal is achieved, the university has the power to operate within a virtually unlimited domain. This power allows UIC to more easily develop collaborative arrangements with community hospitals and other health providers throughout the state.

The importance of this power cannot be overestimated. By establishing a collaborative arrangement with the medical staff of a community hospital, for example, UIC is virtually assured of a regular flow of participants for its programs, many of which are offered on a regular basis in the hospital. The university must secure the greatest amount of intangible resources possible to ensure its long-term survival.

Types of Linkages

The competition for resources among CPE providers in Illinois is extremely intense because of the large number of institutions. The competition for resources is most visible with regard to participants. Intangible resources essential to long-term success in a competitive environment are also pursued, but less openly. Because of the large number of providers, power, prestige, and domain are of central importance to UIC.

Beder explains that success in acquiring resources in a competitive environment requires a strategy. The centerpiece of this strategy is the formation of cooperative relationships with external individuals and organizations capable of supplying the required resources (Beder and Smith, 1977). Four types of relationships are prevalent: cosponsorship, referral, donor, and control-coordination. Cooperative relationships in the CPE program at UIC are ubiquitous. According to the director, "There's not a program we provide that doesn't have at least one of these linkages."

Cosponsorship. A cosponsorship exists when the continuing education unit and an outside agency conduct programs jointly, often on the other cosponsor's premises. Approximately 70 percent of the UIC's 1,500 annual programs are cosponsored. In a recent fiscal year, 124 different health care and community organizations cosponsored programs with UIC, including community hospitals, national professional associations (the American Academy of Family Practice), private industry (G. D. Searle Laboratories), and local groups (Peoria District Dental Society).

Such relationships vary along a continuum of formality and intensity (degree of involvement), and may be grouped into five levels. The least intense level occurs, for example, when the UIC responds to a request from an outside agency to supply a speaker for a program or when UIC requests a mailing list from a professional association for a course offering. The second level occurs if an outside agency wants to offer continuing education credit for a program. In this case, the UIC organizes a formal program-planning process for a one-time program.

At the third level, the UIC staff develop an idea for a program and then join with a number of outside agencies to form a planning committee. This commonly occurs for statewide and national conferences. At the fourth level the UIC and an external agency form a long-term relationship for the delivery of continuing education. This form of linkage exists with a number of community hospitals whereby grand rounds are offered weekly at the hospital. In the final, most formal, type of linkage, a long-term relationship is cemented by a legal contract between the two institutions. Cosponsorship, then, is one way the UIC secures resources from the environment.

Referral. In a referral relationship, an outside agency refers professionals to UIC's continuing education programs. According to the director, all programs in the unit benefit from referral. Yet this type of linkage is almost never formalized. An outside agency may send its employees or urge its members to attend a program because it knows that UIC offers high quality programs in its field. The referral process is encouraged by using speakers well known to outside agencies. For example, one presenter at UIC cardiology programs was on the boards of ten organizations. For these programs, UIC would obtain the ten organizational mailing lists, thus securing a built-in audience. By giving the mailing lists to UIC, these organizations are, in effect, referring their members. As with cosponsorship, referral produces a flow of resources within the environment.

Donor Linkage. A third type of cooperative relationship, donor linkage, exists when another agency donates resources to UIC. This type of linkage is uncommon and, where it exists, is informal. Specifically, 5 percent of the annual budget is derived from monetary gifts, with individual amounts ranging from $100 to $30,000. Usually the money is earmarked for a specific offering, such as "Managerial Skills for Nutrition Services." While this form of linkage is helpful, the program could operate without it. It is not nearly as important as cosponsorship and referral relationships because the major resource obtained is money, a relatively less important resource to UIC.

Control-Coordination. The final type of relationship is control-coordination, whereby personnel from UIC, by virtue of expertise or interest, serve on decision-making bodies of outside agencies, such as the March of Dimes's board of directors. The program planners of UIC have such linkages with many agencies, yet, in the director's words, "You never know how it relates to programming." The effects of this kind of linkage on obtaining tangible resources are indirect. Through control-coordination linkages, planners develop communication networks with others in the field. These networks often provide information helpful in program planning. However, the more important resources garnered through these linkages are intangible. A certain amount of power and prestige is ascribed to the program planners who sit on a board of directors which, in turn, accrues to UIC. The cumulative effect of these intangible resources increases the likelihood that course offerings will be successful.

One of UIC's stated missions is to cooperate with health care agencies and associations in program development. Clearly, the effect of linkages is to vastly increase the amount of resources flowing to the continuing education operation. Interagency collaboration is not established for altruistic reasons, but rather because it facilitates program growth and success. Without collaboration, the program development process would falter. That the linkages are formed for strictly pragmatic reasons is illustrated by the fact that UIC has no linkages with its most natural competitors—other medical school complexes. While UIC will form linkages with almost any other agency, it is in strict competition with other universities. The university medical complexes in UIC's environment share many of the same characteristics that are appealing to other agencies wishing to cooperate with health-related professional schools: a large pool of faculty, an intact program development office, and the ability to offer continuing education credit. The UIC views the situation as a "zero-sum" game in which there is a finite amount of resources in the environment and that those obtained by the other universities are denied to the UIC. Thus the competition for resources. In conclusion, the formation of linkages with external agencies is a highly valued, explicit, and effective approach to securing the resources necessary for the success of the continuing education operation at UIC.

Factors Encouraging External Linkages

What is it about UIC that causes program planners to engage in such substantial interagency collaboration? While no comparative data exist describing the extent of collaborative efforts established by other university continuing education units, it is probably fair to assume that UIC would fall at the higher end of the collaboration continuum. Five factors that appear to be associated with high levels of collaboration are described below.

Type of Instruction. To the extent that the instruction is nonroutine and relatively expensive, program planners will seek more external linkages (Beder, 1978). A large majority of UIC's programs share these characteristics, for they are either one-time programs resulting from the latest medical advances (for example, laser therapy for glaucoma) or programs which may be offered more often but for specialized, limited audiences. In neither case are the programs prepackaged or routine; the same faculty member does not give the same lecture to twenty different groups in a two-month period. Given the low frequency with which any one program is conducted, the costs per program are great, because costs cannot be amortized over many offerings. These characteristics greatly increase the risk of losing money if a course does not succeed in attracting participants. Consequently, reduction of risk is the first reason UIC collaborates with other agencies in the program planning process. Risk is reduced in the following ways when UIC collaborates with professional associations: (1) information regarding members' needs or interests is likely to be accurate and fairly specific; (2) associations expend staff time and other resources in collecting information, expenses that otherwise would have to be borne by UIC; and (3) the number of participants is likely to increase with cosponsorship because the cosponsor further legitimizes the program. Thus, interagency collaboration provides a solid hedge for UIC's risk-taking programming.

Goal Orientation. A second reason for UIC's high level of collaboration is that the mandate for establishing interorganizational relationships is listed among the goals of the agency. Quoting from a recent annual report (Young, 1980): "Is the Medical Campus responding to its mission by cooperating with health care agencies and associations in program development? During fiscal year 1980, the Medical Center Academic Units and Regional Offices cooperated and collaborated with 124 different health care and community organizations to develop and present continuing professional education programs. These organizations provide need assessment information and relate program presentation information to their constituencies. Others approve the program worthy of constituent participation" (p. 6).

In a section dealing with the College of Dentistry, the report states: "The College is committed to working closely with professional societies. The College also works with the Illinois State Dental Society, its component and branch societies, and auxiliary groups to identify needs, to design programs which meet those needs, and to offer programs and evaluate their effectiveness" (p. 69). Finally, the School of Public Health programmers describe their mission: "It is the only public health school in Illinois and is a resource and focal point for scientific inquiry and exchange for and among those professionals whose commonality of concerns allows them to come together in programs for 'public health teams'. The School cooperated with other schools, public health organizations and professional groups in creating [programs] for the multidisciplinary health constituency which is public health" (p. 221). Clearly, the mandate for linkage with external agencies is evident throughout all parts of UIC.

Domain. A third explanatory factor is the extraordinary scope of UIC's domain. The UIC is able to legitimately deal with a large and varied set of institutions. Being part of the largest academic health science center in the country, there is essentially no agency of any size with which the program planners for the six professions could not collaborate. Large collaborating organizations include the World Health Organization, the United Nations, and the United States government. Linkages also exist with much smaller institutions, such as community hospitals and local units of state professional associations. Essentially any agency that has an interest in health care is a potential linkage partner.

Resource Security. A fourth reason for UIC's high level of collaboration is the desire to secure an uninterrupted flow of resources. This is accomplished through a two-pronged strategy. The principle behind the strategy is that by creating a large and diverse number of interorganizational linkages, UIC increases its autonomy by reducing its dependency on any one source of resource supply. The first part of the strategy is to become part of an interdependent network of CPE providers. In this way both tangible and intangible resources will flow to the UIC on a constant basis. As the director noted: "There's not any one cosponsorship relationship that is necessary for UIC to continue its operation." The second part of the strategy involves maintaining the flow of resources from the parent body, the university as a whole. "Every institution has an Achilles heel which continuing education is expected to protect," the director stated, "and to the extent you successfully protect it, your flow of resources from the parent body is secured." The Achilles' heel of the University of Illinois is its own hospital, which has a surplus of bed spaces. Beds are filled by referral from primary and secondary care physicians. This partially explains why most graduate faculty will work on a continuing education program for no fee. Another more complex relationship exists in a medium-sized city in another part of the state. The two hospitals in that city expend a fair amount of resources to help the university educate its medical students and residents. The UIC continuing education program uses those hospitals' specialists as faculty, thus increasing the number of referrals to those hospitals. This, in turn, helps the hospitals remain solvent so that they will be able to support the university's medical school training and residency programs. The parent body values these arrangements; thus, it is likely to continue an uninterrupted flow of resources from the University to the continuing education unit.

Environmental Characteristics. Environmental characteristics comprise the final variable determining high level of collaboration. Environments that are dynamic and that have a high organizational density are especially conducive to a high level of interagency collaboration. The UIC presents an interesting situation because programming is done both in a highly dynamic and organizationally dense location, Chicago, and in other areas of the state where the environment is relatively stable and has fewer possible linkage partners. Yet the director reports similarly high levels of collaboration throughout the state. He explains that collaboration is necessary, regardless of the environmental conditions, to obtain some of the tangible resources—information, participants, and facilities—and all of the intangible resources—power, prestige, and domain. The intangibles, he believes, can be obtained only through collaboration, for they cannot be purchased or donated by others.

It would be difficult to sort out the relative importance of these five factors in explaining UIC's high level of collaboration. They appear to work together to promote a multiplicity of linkages with external agencies for program development. For example, the goal orientation of the agency coupled with a virtually unlimited domain results in a large number of linkages which help to maintain the agency's autonomy and uninterrupted flow of resources. In truth, the interactions among these factors are so complex that an exhaustive description is impossible.

Cost/Benefit Ratio of Interagency Collaboration

Thus far in the presentation of the UIC case study, three of the questions initally posed have been discussed:
1. What resources does the agency seek from the environment?
2. What types of linkages does the agency form with its environment to obtain these resources?
3. What factors help explain the extent to which UIC has formed linkages?

The fourth question, "What are the costs and benefits of these linkages to the agency?" is the final focus of this chapter. Reflecting upon discussion of the first three questions, it may seem as though the formation of organizational linkages would solve any program development problem that could conceivably arise. The realistic reader might be skeptical, however, and with good reason. There are, indeed, costs as well as benefits involved in the development and maintenance of interagency linkages. Yet if the benefits and costs are compared, one can easily see why the continuing education unit of UIC aggressively pursues linkages with external agencies. Examination of the director's assessment of costs and benefits forms the basis of response to the fourth question. Benefits fall into three categories: recruitment of participants, support of the parent body, and visibility. Potential problems that can arise from collaboration include loss of autonomy, organizational disruption, and termination of linkage.

By forming referral and cosponsorship linkages, UIC greatly increases the likelihood of recruiting a sufficient number of participants for their programs. Evidence of the success of this strategy is an extremely low program cancellation rate. Typically, fewer than ten programs from a possible 1,500 are cancelled annually because of insufficient enrollment. In addition, recruitment accomplished through referral and cosponsorship does not require any extra expenditure of UIC's funds.

A second crucial benefit that results from long-term collaborative arrangements, particularly those with community hospitals, is the ongoing support of the parent body. This support derives from ongoing patient referrals made by continuing medical education program participants. While referrals do not directly support the continuing education program, the indirect result from full utilization of hospital services by clientele is revenue. It is revenue which ultimately affects the ability of the total university system to provide programs and services through all its units or agencies.

A final major benefit of collaboration is the visibility inherent in regular contact with co-collaborators. Of course, the major result of this visibility is an extension of UIC's domain. The importance of this intangible resource has been stressed repeatedly: in the director's words, "You want to create in the minds of external agencies and individuals that you are a legitimate provider of CPE."

In comparison to the benefits, the costs of developing collaborative arrangements, according to the director, are minimal. While these arrangements cause UIC to relinquish some autonomy in program development, the director considers this to be positive because he believes interdependence is much more practical than independence. He does not believe an institution could survive by going it alone in CPE program development. Another reason loss of autonomy is no problem is related to UIC's cultivation of numerous and diverse linkages. The UIC is not dependent on any one partner. Thus, if a partner were to make demands in the development of a specific program that

UIC could not accommodate, UIC could afford to terminate the relationship.

The second potential problem, organizational disruption, has been a reality for UIC. Specific examples include failure on the part of the collaborating agency to advertise a cosponsored program in their membership newsletters and failure to complete timely mailings of program publicity to potential participants. Similarly, a collaborating partner, who was responsible for reviewing the final copy for a brochure, not only submitted the copy after the deadline but also requested numerous changes. Obviously, the lesson here is that it takes more time and energy to develop and implement a cosponsored program than to develop the same program alone.

The final potential problem involves the ramifications of linkage termination. Consequences such as jeopardized relationships and negative image are realistic concerns. However, UIC has had to terminate only one formal linkage and this was done by mutual agreement. In sum, the only significant cost to the UIC of interagency linkages has been organizational disruption. Given these relative costs and benefits of interagency collaboration, is it any wonder that linkage is a major component of UIC's program development process?

Conclusions and Implications

For UIC, interorganizational collaboration in program development is not consummated because it is theoretically or politically "incorrect." Rather, these relationships are a key strategy in the agency's immediate and long-term program development efforts. For the short-term (that is, developing 1,500 annual programs), the linkages provide information about participants' needs and interests, an available pool of learners, and conveniently located facilities. In the long run, the intangible resources gained from the linkages—power, prestige, domain—provide a secure foundation for the growth of the agency. If any agency engaged in CPE must obtain resources because it is not fully supported by its parent body, it should seek to form collaborative arrangements with external agencies.

Since UIC staff, several of whom hold doctorates in continuing education, are capable of planning quality programs with internal resources alone, improving progam quality as not cited by the director as a reason for collaboration. Rather, impetus is provided by the need to effectively deliver the programs. Many high quality programs have been cancelled because the location was inconvenient or the potential learners were unaware of the program. Interorganizational linkages are an effective strategy to increase the likelihood that the right types of participants are aware of the right programs offered at convenient locations.

Throughout this chapter, collaboration has been viewed from a sociological perspective, thus underemphasizing the personal dimension involved in the collaboration process. The personal dimension is essential. The director emphasized that a major criterion he uses in selecting staff is their ability to get along with and communicate with others. Individual people are responsible for developing and maintaining successful interorganizational linkages. These linkages, however, endure beyond the tenure of an individual. Institutions support collaborative efforts because they function in the achievement of the fundamental purposes of the institution.

References

Beder, H. W. "An Environmental Interaction Model for Agency Development in Adult Education." *Adult Education,* 1978, *28,* 176-190.

Beder, H. W., and Smith, F. *Program Development in Adult Education Through Community Linkages.* New York: Center for Adult Education, Columbia University, Teachers College, 1977.

Benson, J. "The Interorganizational Network as a Political Economy." *Administrative Science Quarterly,* 1975, *21,* 229-249.

Berlin, L. S. "The University and Continuing Professional Education: A Contrary View." In M. R. Stern (Ed.), *Power and Conflict in Continuing Professional Education.* Belmont, Calif.: Wadsworth, 1983.

Davies, H. M., and Aquino, J. T. "Collaboration in Continuing Professional Development." *Journal of Teacher Education,* 1975, *26,* 274-277.

Hohmann, L. "How Can the Professional Association and Other Providers Best Interact?" In P. E. Frandson (Ed.), *Power and Conflict in Continuing Education.* Belmont, Calif.: Wadsworth, 1980.

Houle, C. O. *Continuing Learning in the Professions.* San Francisco: Jossey-Bass, 1980.

Knox, A. B. "Organizational Dynamics in University Continuing Professional Education." *Adult Education,* 1982, *32,* 117-129.

Manning, P. R., and others. "Continuing Medical Education: Linking the Community Hospital and the Medical School." *Journal of Medical Education,* 1979, *54,* 461-466.

Nowlen, P. N., and Stern, M. R. "Partnerships in Continuing Education for Professionals." In *Partnerships with Business and the Professions.* 1981 Current Issues in Higher Education. American Association for Higher Education, 1981.

Shelton, H. R., and Craig, R. L. "Continuing Professional Development: The Employer's Perspective." In M. R. Stern (Ed.), *Power and Conflict in Continuing Professional Education.* Belmont, Calif.: Wadsworth, 1983.

Stern, M. R. (Ed.). *Power and Conflict in Continuing Professional Education.* Belmont, Calif.: Wadsworth, 1983.

Suleiman, A. "Private Enterprise: The Independent Provider." In M. R. Stern (Ed.), *Power and Conflict in Continuing Professional Education.* Belmont, Calif.: Wadsworth, 1983.

Young, W. H. *University of Illinois at the Medical Center, Continuing Professional Education Report, Fiscal Year 1980.* Chicago: University of Illinois, 1980.

Younghouse, R. H. *A National Study of Cosponsored Continuing Medical Education Category One Programming Activities Between Medical Schools and Community Hospitals.* Unpublished doctoral dissertation, University of Illinois at Urbana-Champaign, 1983.

Ronald M. Cervero is assistant professor of adult education, Northern Illinois University, and teaches graduate courses on continuing professional education. Previously he was assistant director of the Illinois Council on Continuing Professional Education.

"The power company was really looking for a product, and the university was looking for a relationship."

Who's in Control? A Case Study of University-Industry Collaboration

Arlene Fingeret

Are nuclear power plants safe? This question haunts the nuclear power industry as well as the general public, and has heightened interest in nuclear power plant operator training. The Nuclear Regulatory Commission (NRC) has required an upgrading of training programs and is closely monitoring the industry's response to its problems. Utilities have created the Institute for Nuclear Power Operations (INPO) as a mechanism for improving training throughout the industry. In addition, many utilities have sought to supplement their technical expertise through cooperative arrangements with educational institutions for the design and implementation of educational programs.

The Case Study Approach

This is the story of one such collaborative effort between a team from a large American university (LAU) and a utility, anonymously referred to here as the power company (TPC). The goal of their cooperation was the development of a new training program which would provide the nuclear power plant operators with the background necessary to respond appropriately in emergency situations. University continuing education administered the program. The project director came from the department of nuclear engineering, and team members represented adult education, chemistry, mathematics, physics, mechanical engineering, and health physics.

The topic of collaboration between industry and universities is not new. Recent economic circumstances have further heightened interest in such efforts. The difficulties generally encountered in such collaborative undertakings are widely documented, but often they are oversimplified by being presented out of context. In order to present as richly woven a tapestry as possible, I individually interviewed sixteen of the major actors from both the university and the utility, and analyzed the documents they have produced. Each interview was tape recorded and lasted a minimum of one hour, with many lasting much longer. Three key persons were interviewed a second time. Five respondents who played major roles in the project reviewed earlier drafts of this manuscript for accuracy and plausability of the interpretive analysis.

The remainder of this chapter is organized into three sections. The project is described in Part One. It is set into a larger framework in Part Two. Although the project lasted only one year, it is used to illustrate the powerful impact of environmental forces over which neither organization had control. It also provides insight into many of the concepts often used by theorists of interorganizational behavior, such as domain, authority, resources, tradition, and values. In Part Three, I have formulated principles for cooperative relationships and have identified ways that future cooperative efforts may benefit from the experience related here.

Part One: The Project

The Teams. Morton was vice president for nuclear operations, TPC, at the time this project was initiated. His corporate office team included Frankel, director of training services; Hirsch, supervisor of training development; and Davis, manager of nuclear operations. Before the completion of the project, Morton was promoted to senior vice president for engineering; Davis was promoted to vice president of nuclear operations; and Frankel took a one year leave to work at INPO, although he has now returned to TPC as director of nuclear training.

The university team was directed by Mills, director of the school of engineering's nuclear reactor training program, and the project was administered by Smithfield, assistant vice-chancellor for continuing education. Mills's team included Longstreet, director of the school of engineering's industrial extension service; Corey, professor of chemistry; Appel, professor of mathematics; and Curry, professor of adult education.

The names of the organizations and the individuals have been changed to protect their identities; everyone I approached, however, claimed that confidentiality was not of major concern. They all view industry-university relationships as both important and problematic.

Rationale for Collaboration. The NRC regulates utilities operating nuclear power plants. In March, 1980, the NRC issued a set of documents in which it describes its revised criteria for reactor operator training and licensing. The proposed revision to the qualifications of operators, which carries no implementation deadline, reads:

1. Shift supervisors shall have an engineering degree or equivalent qualifications.
2. Senior operators shall have successfully completed a course in appropriate engineering and scientific subjects equal to 60 credit hours of college level subjects (Deuton, 1980, p. 6).

Although this section is titled "Long Range Criteria and/or Requirements" and is prefaced with the comment that such requirements need "additional staff work and/or rule making prior to... implementation," the cover letter urges utilities to start planning for these new requirements as soon as possible. University degrees represented a new orientation for the NRC, and the potential new regulations heightened utilities' interest in a cooperative relationship with a university.

TPC administrators claim that the proposed regulations were part of their reason for approaching LAU, but that they also felt a professional responsibility for upgrading the training. Davis (vice-president for nuclear operations, TPC) describes traditional industry training programs as "mundane kinds of things" and "not the state of the art." Morton, vice-president for nuclear operations at the time this project was initiated, hired a continuing educator to assist TPC in improving its training program for reactor operators. Morton found himself learning more than he had anticipated:

> One of the first things we did was a job task analysis. I didn't think the job task analysis was going to be useful. I think all of us were sitting around telling ourselves that we knew what people did. We felt like we were being asked to do an academic exercise—we were willing to do it, but it took some convincing on my part, at least. In actual fact, we found it very valuable.

> We found out that we had a training program that, at best, would not really train them for all the jobs they had to do.

Convinced that the academic world had something to offer, Morton started investigating cooperative relationships with educational institutions. "We'll sell you anything we have but we're not going to develop something new" typifies the response he received from local community colleges and universities. He wanted something developed specifically for TPC.

In August, 1981, a group of TPC senior officials was attending a meeting at LAU to discuss cooperative research when they heard a presentation about the nuclear reactor training program LAU operates. "What can you do for us?" someone asked Anderson, chairperson of nuclear engineering at LAU. Anderson replied that LAU might be interested in developing an educational program for reactor operators, and asked Mills, the director of the reactor training program, to follow up. Mills recently had joined the faculty, following ten years in the utility industry. Mills wrote a short report on the work he had been doing through LAU for other utility companies and sent it to TPC. Morton (vice-president, nuclear operations) asked Mills if they could set up a meeting to discuss the possibility of a cooperative project.

Mills talked to Smithfield, the assistant vice-chancellor for continuing education, and officials of TPC and LAU finally met at the university's Continuing Education Center in October 1981. They spent the morning touring the center and, following lunch, spent the afternoon in an exploratory meeting, described by Smithfield as follows:

> We talked from lunch till about four, and for the last thirty minutes, Morton said, "Can LAU come in and evaluate our program, propose courses for us and outline delivery system, and even be involved in delivering those, down the road?" Then he asked about how much it would cost. Our response was yes, we could do studies, we could look at delivery systems, we could design course outlines, [and] courses.... And that there probably could be some way we could be involved, but at that point we didn't know just what was needed and how much we could actually be involved....

Morton (vice-president, TPC) reveals his surprise at the university position:

> They were guarded about their enthusiasm for jumping into this until they knew more about it. If I'd been talking to a con-

sultant, no matter what I might have said he'd have been extremely enthusiastic and he'd be making me quotations right and left. I was prepared to go down there with a problem and to hear a solution—with a price tag on it.

During the following two months, while TPC officials discussed the possibility of this cooperative venture, Mills and Smithfield tentatively began to form a team to work on the project. They identified and recruited individuals from as broad a range of related disciplines as possible, including chemistry, physics, health physics, and engineering.

Curry, for example, was a professor of education. He had extensive experience with extension education and a personal interest in this project.

Corey was the assistant department chairperson in chemistry at that time. His wife works at a local utility and had extensive contact with Mills. As a result of her description, Corey was interested in working with Mills. In addition, Corey grew up near one of the first nuclear power plants and had a personal interest in that industry. Although he felt that the project was "pretty nebulous" and he had no prior industrial experience, Corey agreed to serve as the chemistry member of the team.

Appel, a mathematics professor, had been teaching extension mathematics courses in industrial settings for almost fifteen years. He found the extra income useful since he has five children and "they have to go to college." Appel has been developing a computer-assisted interactive video instruction (CAVI) program for introductory undergraduate mathematics courses at LAU. Mills thought such a system might be useful to TPC, and included Appel on the team.

And what of Mills himself? As a graduate student he had felt that the faculty lacked important industrial experience; when he returned to the university he felt isolated because of his years in industry. However, "within the extension side of the university, I felt a lot of warmth," Mills reports. The project team valued Mills's industrial experience and provided him with collegial relationships lacking elsewhere.

Getting Started. Both university continuing education and TPC decided they were interested in continuing to explore this potential collaborative effort, and Mills received a Request for Proposal (RFP) from TPC on November 30, 1982. The RFP outlined the task as "evaluation of [power plant] nonplant specific subjects;" specifically LAU is to "evaluate the content of the subjects we now teach relative to what, from an academic viewpoint, we should be teaching." TPC invited the university team to visit one of its nuclear power plants as part of its preparation for writing the proposal, and the tour was arranged.

The day before the trip, Mills met with his department's faculty. Even though this project and Mills's involvement had been in response to a direct request from the chairperson of the nuclear engineering department, Mills found that most of the senior faculty had had negative experiences with utilities and were far from supportive of this new venture. According to Mills, "[They] told me that I could not represent the department, that I must take this on as a consultant.... They said, 'Oh, TPC is just trying to use our good name, and you can't teach those operators.'"

"[The utility] didn't support our academic programs with scholarship funds, they didn't support our research program and everyone looked at them and said, 'Why should we do something for you? What's in it for us?'" explains Anderson, the department chairperson. The faculty discussed whether the status of Mills's work for the utility should be release time ("part of the academic mission of the department") or consulting. Anderson asserts that the final decision, consulting, reflects the fact that, "In this department there is only one recognized legitimate activity besides academics, and that's sponsored research... not educational program development."

Mills did not allow the sentiments of the rest of the nuclear engineering faculty to interfere with the next day's trip. The team spent the day at the power plant meeting with the training staff and learning about TPC's operator training program. The morning was uncomfortable, however. Corey (Chemistry, LAU) reported, "[We] got a very distinct feeling that the training people were sort of caught by surprise. They didn't know quite what to think and were a little bit cautious, and I can't blame them in the least bit. They got the idea that things had been stirred up from up above and they didn't know what we were going to do and we didn't know how they were going to fit into things." Morton (vice-president, TPC) joined the meeting around noon and, according to Smithfield (continuing education, LAU) "in essence turned the whole thing around, it was as different as night and day because he not only told [the trainers] why [we were there], he said, 'We need education wrapped around the training.'"

The teams explored what the utility company wanted from the project. Hirsch (new supervisor, training development, TPC) wanted text materials that operator candidates could use for study, and he wanted the materials to be pragmatic. Discussion ensued about how Hirsch's specifications relate to the NRC's proposed requirement for college level study. "There was a difference of opinion about what ['college level'] meant," recalls Hirsch. Although the university team left the meeting feeling that some kind of consensus had been achieved, differences of opinion would continue to plague the project.

The University's Proposal. Following the meeting the university team, directed by Mills, developed and submitted a proposal to TPC. They conceived two phases for the project: the first for identifying needs and exploring alternatives, and the second for actually developing and implementing a new training program. In the proposal, which was accepted by TPC, they agreed to fulfill the following objectives, which were related to Phase One only:

1. To identify areas where the existing non–plant-specific training materials being used at the TPC... power plants for training reactor operators may be improved by making specific revisions to that material.
2. To identify and outline academic courses that would give the reactor operator the education necessary to understand the reactor fundamentals that underlie the training materials now being presented by the TPC staff.
3. To provide practical alternatives for the packaging and delivery of educational material to the operations personnel.

Phase One. The project quickly became known as the "TPC Feasibility Study" and a timeline from March 15 to December 15, 1982 was established. The project was administered by university continuing education, and the chairperson of every department involved was provided with a copy of the proposal. All chairpersons were asked to sign forms agreeing to the involvement of their designated faculty members, and identifying whether the funds were to be paid directly to the faculty member or to the department to support releasing the work time of the individual. Every department chairperson signed a form; all nine-month employees received the funds directly. Twelve-month employees, with the exception of the project director (Mills), received regular work time to participate in the project. This means that in the case of all faculty other than those in adult education, continuing education (for instance, general extension), and industrial extension, this project was identified as consulting. During this period, Mills and Hirsch acted as liaisons for the university and the utility respectively.

The University Analyzes Its Task. Mills recognized that some members of his team had neither industrial experience nor experience with nuclear power plants. Therefore, he developed work teams consisting of faculty members paired with undergraduate students who were ex-Navy nuclear personnel and were working in the regular reactor training program. These students assisted the faculty in understanding the demands of a reactor operator's job.

The task facing the university team still was not clear, as one faculty member explained: "I must say, we floundered for several months, wondering, 'Am I supposed to figure out what to put in this thing for two days, or am I supposed to figure out how long it's going to take to teach what I think they need to know?'"

Each faculty team member was faced with the dual task of determining appropriate content as well as delivery mode. Content had to be organized so that all of the topics deemed necessary were covered, and so that the material from each discipline was integrated. A physics course that required specific mathematics skills had to be coordinated with the math curriculum. In addition, the overall curriculum had to allow operators to remain on their jobs while studying at the plant site.

Smithfield (continuing education, LAU) and Mills visited the NRC and INPO (the industry's organization charged with improving training) to procure additional information about the regulations and guidelines to which TPC's program had to conform. The NRC, they discovered, was waiting to see what INPO would do. INPO had developed a set of course content guidelines which Smithfield and Mills were able to procure through pre-existing relationships with INPO personnel. The guidelines were passed on to the project faculty and used to guide the curriculum development work.

In addition to educating themselves about the INPO guidelines and NRC regulations, the team was concerned with modes of delivery and with addressing the special needs of adult learners. Curry (adult education, LAU) and Longstreet (industrial extension, LAU) had extensive experience in continuing education, and they were asked to provide a seminar on adult learning and instructional systems for the university and industry teams. To prepare, Curry visited one of the utility's power plants. "I talked to Hirsch and the training person there, and there sure were some apparent discrepancies between what Hirsch said that TPC wanted and what Mills understood they wanted in talking to their superior at TPC. Mills and Smithfield had been negotiating with the top dogs, and these [training personnel] were all middle management.... When I came back and said to Mills, 'Do you realize that...' he would say, 'You don't understand that I have been talking to the vice-president.'"

The work progressed steadily. Mills and members of his team met periodically with Hirsch (supervisor, training development, TPC) to check on the status of the work. Anderson (chairperson, nuclear engineering, LAU) was kept apprised of the project's progress. Anderson felt that LAU's interests were not well represented. "Mills got very much involved with Smithfield," Anderson asserted, "and Smithfield is candidly out to maximize the dollar income to continuing education." Mills, therefore, found himself in an increasingly difficult position: He was enjoying extension work but was being evaluated by his academic colleagues. He found that his activities had no place on the annual faculty reporting forms.

Other university team members found it easier to reconcile their regular faculty responsibilities with their roles in the project. They and their departments were not as extensively identified with the project as were Mills and nuclear engineering. In addition, the project provided resources specifically desired by some departments. For example, TPC paid for a computer programmer to work with Appel to develop the CAVI lessons. Appel published an article about his work in a professional journal, drawing the attention of other universities. He found his department chairperson very supportive of the TPC project; it brought in overhead money and exposure to the "real world" as well as support for the CAVI development. Smithfield (continuing education, LAU) saw the project as a major opportunity for service as well as for providing summer employment for faculty. He found the deans cooperative, except for one case: "[The dean of the school of engineering] was committed to doing this type of thing, but he would have probably been happier if it had been a research project."

University/Industry Conflict. Despite internal university problems, relationships with TPC training staff had to be maintained. One major issue began to surface consistently: Who is in control of the level of the content in the proposed courses? Each team felt professionally responsible for defining the final product and this led to an impasse. TPC wanted training curricula specifically addressing the job task analysis they had completed. They felt that the professors were unwilling to respect TPC's analysis of its training needs: "'I know better than you what you need.' I heard that many times, and I didn't like hearing it even once. Repetition only made it worse.... Somewhere along the line, we got the idea that the university had the upper hand, and we resented it—the people at my level doing the work. The academicians, they only see one way. 'I did it that way, that's the standard curriculum, and that's the way everyone's going to do it'" (Hirsch, supervisor, training development, TPC).

The professors, on the other hand, felt that they had been asked to make a professional assessment of the situation and that now they had to promote their ideas to TPC. Appel (mathematics, LAU) comments: "Being university professors, you just can't help but be as general as you can get away with in the process of developing materials. You try to do it professionally, which means you try not to take too many short cuts."

The LAU team attempted to respond to TPC's criticism by showing them the differences between the proposed curriculum and the regular university courses, but the conflict persisted. According to one team member, "It wasn't that people wanted to get a personal profit from this, it really was control in the sense of making sure that it was done right." The university group wanted to insure that the integrity of the disciplines was maintained, while TPC had to insure an uninterrupted flow of electric power, which placed limits on operators' time and the depth of the content. In the words of one professor: "[TPC] was really looking for a product, and the university was, I think, looking for a relationship."

It appears that these issues—control of content, time frame, and delivery mode—never were fully resolved. A preliminary report was issued in August 1982, and the university and industry teams met to review the work. Anderson (chairperson, nuclear engineering, LAU) and Bracier (dean, school of engineering) also attended that meeting because they had the impression from the preliminary report that LAU was making a commitment to Phase II, implementation. They did not want to make that commitment and they learned at the meeting, to their relief, that TPC expected to maintain full control over Phase II options.

Smithfield felt that "Morton (vice-president, TPC) seemed to think he was getting what he wanted," and that the preliminary Phase I report had received approval. However, the same conflicts also arose at this meeting: "Frankel (director of training services, TPC) and maybe some of the other folks felt that [the courses] were too deep. But in discussing it, we said these touched all the points of the INPO guidelines and what the faculty feel coming out of the disciplines is appropriate to apply to the industry in that area. So Frankel's position was, 'Well, go ahead.'. . . So we did" (Smithfield).

"Maybe I didn't communicate clearly enough," is Frankel's response. He continued, "We knew what we wanted and Dr. Tom [Mills] knew what he wanted, and really there was no meeting of the minds even though Mills went away saying, 'OK, we'll give you what you want,' because that's not what we got." Hirsch adds that LAU's use of the INPO guidelines may have compounded the problems. INPO guidelines were being revised constantly, but he felt that the university treated the existing guidelines "as though they were edicts."

The Phase One Report. The university team, apparently believing it had received the go-ahead and had convinced the industry training staff to support its proposed courses, proceeded to develop the final report. The original draft postulated LAU involvement in the actual writing and implementation of the courses described. At the insistence of the dean of the school of engineering, the proposal was amended to reflect more general Phase II alternatives. Bracier wanted to make sure that faculty were not obligated to implement Phase II and that TPC was not obligated to LAU. He explains: "Our faculty are hired to teach and their primary missions are undergraduate teaching and scholarship. Neither of these would have been served [in Phase II, which] is an extension type program." After circulation to team members and departmental administrators, the report was revised and submitted.

The Phase I report contained proposed training program course outlines and descriptions of the strengths and limitations of various educational technologies for delivering the material. It also contained an assessment of the time and money that would be required for LAU to produce the courses, that is, to implement Phase II. The budget, totalling millions of dollars, included funds for developing video production studio facilities. The courses were to be "bits and pieces out of the undergraduate curriculum" (Corey, chemistry, LAU) rather than the plant-specific curricula TPC requested. "I bent to meet their needs," claims Appel (mathematics, LAU). "But I would make sure that in the process enough was thrown in there to make sure that [the operators] knew what was going on."

In the interval between the final meeting and actual submission of the report, Morton was reassigned within the company and a new vice president for nuclear operations, Davis, was named. In addition, Frankel was assigned to a twelve-month rotation at INPO. The audience for the final report, therefore, was different from the team for which it had been prepared.

The university team hoped to have the opportunity to discuss the report with the utility team, as they had done for previous drafts. Instead of a commitment for a meeting, however, they received a letter from Davis thanking them for their efforts, and concluding; "We believe that high technology training methods must definitely be a part of our training strategy, but that the use of the faculty and staff of your university to prepare such programs is not now a cost effective or timely avenue of approach to meet our objectives." Smithfield believes that the response might have been different if Morton was still the vice-president for nuclear operations. Morton "wanted a long and continuing relationship with the university," according to Smithfield (continuing education, LAU). "When he's gone, the new people have no commitment; this was not their idea."

Davis (new vice-president, nuclear operations, TPC) did not share Smithfield's view. He was involved in the project from the beginning in his capacity as manager of nuclear operations and would have been involved in evaluating the report even if his position had not changed. His evaluation:

> The subject matter in the course outlines went far beyond what we were trying to accomplish in certain areas. We got the feeling these guys want to finance other things they want to do, and charge it to TPC. [They'd] build facilities, and we'd pick up the capital costs for those facilities. I don't mind helping out the university—we do plenty of that. But for a particular proposal, we expect a certain amount for our money, completely outside helping out the university. We certainly like to do that when we can. But the universities want you to buy what they already do rather than try to work with you and tailor something to what your needs are, like any other contractor would do... and I'm not singling out LAU for this.

Hirsch (supervisor, training development, TPC) found the sections on instructional technology useful, but not the course content. He questioned the university's view of the report as a step in a relationship rather than a final product. "Why, after a whole year of haranguing, was the comment made. 'Well, of course we'll revise the outlines to meet what you want.'? What was the point of that? Why did it take a year for that to happen? We could have been much more productive. That's why I say, up front we should agree about what we're going to do. And maybe the utility was partly at fault for not being more assertive."

Money aside, TPC's decision to terminate its relationship with LAU with the completion of Phase I, rather than to continue with Phase II, appears to center around two major issues: dissatisfaction with the actual course content proposed by the university team and with the stipulated time frame of three years. "Our schedule is the calendar year, not the academic year," reflects Morton (vice-president, TPC). "We had to learn that our schedules are different."

Many of the participants relate the issue of appropriateness of course content to their views of education and training. The university team felt that they were engaged in developing an educational program and that their mandate for education, rather than training, came from the NRC. Those from industry also felt they were looking for education, but tempered by the realities of the work setting. "I came to TPC with these lofty ideals about what should be done—I'm an educator, not a trainer," asserts Hirsch.

Was the proposed curriculum education or training? As might be expected, such a question is difficult to answer. The chairperson of nuclear engineering felt, "It looked very cookbookish. That, to me, gets more into training—when you memorize stuff rather than understand it—and our faculty are not involved in training." Hirsch, in contrast, saw the proposed curriculum as "university level education."

Since the curriculum modules were described, but samples were not actually developed, it is difficult to get a clear understanding of the level of the proposed curriculum. The university team appears to have been caught between their feelings of responsibility to their disciplines, which disaffected TPC, and the utility's demand for time limitations, which alienated the chairperson of nuclear engineering.

Current Assessments. Smithfield (continuing education, LAU) believes the project has been completed: "We successfully did what we set out to do. As we worked on it, Mills was positive we'd develop and implement those courses, but that wasn't what we set out to do. We gave them the course outlines and they can take them anywhere."

The chairperson of nuclear engineering (Anderson) believes that any department role in Phase II would have to be defined very carefully. LAU could have a legitimate role "writing text materials, producing some videotapes, or perhaps working with a community college, helping them implement this." Offering the training program itself, however, would involve providing "an Associate Degree type program at best," which he considers inappropriate for LAU. Anderson stated:

> We have two major missions and a minor. One of the major ones is the educational mission, whether it be undergraduate or graduate. Another major mission is contributions toward applied and basic research in engineering in the broadest sense, and it's very broad. And then the minor mission that we have is one of extension. I know we're supposed to do these three things, but the reality is we don't have the resources to do them all, so extension is a minor mission. We try to do it as best we can.

Bracier (dean, school of engineering, LAU) expands:

> As engineers, we are interested in transferring technology, and the people who develop that technology and carry it to the public are generally found in industries, so I think that the extension role is always going to be a challenge for us and the most difficult one for us to wrestle with.... The role of exten-

sion is different. We can just commit ourselves to do it independently of our other obligations—and you're just going to end up with a lot of difficult situations. If you say we really ought to be an organization that is "pure," we're not supposed to get involved in social and industrial issues—that's equally hard to do.

Those from the utility, however, are not concerned with whether the university considers it appropriate to engage in Phase II. They are continuing their efforts to comply with NRC guidelines, and are now working with a local community college and another university.

They try to put into practice the lessons they feel they learned from their relationship with LAU. "We go in very clear about what we want, reiterated each time. We meet with faculty. The faculty will not be paid until the material meets the requirements of TPC and the college. And it's not that we're trying to be mean—we want everyone to understand right up front what we want, and we'll get what we want."

Hirsch believes that universities should retain their academic standards, but that faculty must recognize that these standards do not necessarily apply to industrial training programs. Faculty must understand that "the people they are preparing materials for are different from themselves." Hirsch thinks that the effort made to teach project faculty about continuing education when Curry, the adult education professor, was brought in was not sufficient.

INPO has continued its work and "came around closer to the side of the industry than the university," according to Hirsch. He concludes, "Maybe it was unfortunate that we got caught in our negotiation at that time when there was a big gap between what INPO was recommending and what the utility wanted."

Recently, TPC has been employing more educators. "These are practical people, not academics," in Frankel's (director of training services, TPC) estimation. The educators work together with technical personnel to develop curriculum. Frankel thinks TPC is in good shape: "Between the training systems development effort that INPO has put forth and the job task analysis that TPC has done, we can now pretty well define what it is that the individual needs to know, identify the terminal learning objectives and the job performance measures, and actually go out and evaluate an individual against the standards."

TPC officers have become cautious in relationships with universities. Morton (vice-president, TPC) finds that now he approaches meetings with "outsiders" differently: "The first thing that I ask myself is, 'What is the problem?' And I can't just answer it with something like, 'I'm trying to improve the training program.' I have to ask what it is about the training program that I want to see different."

"It's a rigorous trail to get anything meaty. We spend months and months talking to university people and having meetings — it's arduous. And very little happens," summarizes Davis (new vice-president, nuclear operations, TPC) about relationships in general with universities for provision of educational programs. TPC has a variety of existing relationships with universities for research as well as "an interest in the general good, and in providing assistance where we can to the universities." But when it comes to universities developing specific programs for TPC, Davis claims, "it hasn't filled our needs."

The Project Director. Mills consistently is identified by both the university and industry teams as central to the project. The university team felt he could speak industry's language and, therefore, was a good choice for project director. His department chairperson (Anderson), however, did not see this quality as an asset. "It would have been better if Mills had been a little more academic. There wasn't much in common between his interests and the faculty's. If there would have been a person up there who was a first-class researcher whom the faculty had accepted as a colleague, who then decided to do this, I think they would have gone with it because they would have trusted the individual, but that wasn't the case." And the members of the industry team see Mills as too tightly connected to the university and unable to understand or respond to industry's needs. In Hirsch's words: "Perhaps Mills understood the language of industry and could speak the language of industry, but I heard him speaking the language of the university."

By the time Phase I was completed, Mills was approaching professional review by his department and he was faced with some difficult choices. Mills entered the university expecting that his industrial management skills would be applicable and rewarded in this new context. Instead, he found that his dual appointment as director of the nuclear training program and associate professor was to be evaluated by the faculty according to academic criteria. "I didn't realize what that would mean," Mills comments. "I walked right into it, and I had nobody to help me." Mills's work with industry did not lend itself to research or graduate student support. When it was classified as consulting, Mills reflected, "I didn't really understand what that meant." Finally, according to Mills, "I was told I had to do research by the first of the year, or I was not going to be reappointed. There was no way I could stay in the university . . . with that kind of lack of support for something I thought was so important, so I left."

Part Two: Discussion

Overview. This is a complex tale of a group of intelligent, respected professional educators who responded in good faith to a request for assistance from a large utility company. In the process, they appear to have alienated the utility's training personnel and have incurred some disfavor among the administrators of the school of engineering. In order to develop deeper insight into the problems encountered, this section analyzes the project as an example of a loosely coupled interorganizational system. The utility's and the university's concern with survival is fundamental to this perspective of organizations and cooperation. Many authors translate that concern into a direct interest in procurement of resources from the external environment (see Yuchtman and Seashore, 1967).

One mechanism for procuring resources is the development of linkages with other organizations that affect, in some way, the flow of resources. When linkage occurs, the organizations may be classified as interdependent; this means, to use Litwak and Rothman's (1970, p. 147) definition, "that two or more organizations must take each other into account in order to best achieve their individual goals.... The acts of one organization affect those of another in an immediate way." In this project each organization preserves its separate identity and there is a clear, logical, and physical differentiation between them. This type of interdependence is known as *loose coupling*.

Both the utility and the university belong to extensive networks, or multiple networks, of organizations. Each organization's network operates within the larger social context, which includes other networks and organizations with which there may not be direct interaction, but those actions may influence those networks with which we are directly concerned in this project (Emery and Trist, 1965). Pfeffer and Salancik (1978) describe three levels of the environment: the entire system of interconnected organizations and individuals; that set with which an organization interacts directly; and the organization's perception and representation of its environment. This last level, labeled the *enacted environment*, is of concern here. Decisions will be made in organizations on the basis of the selective observation, perception, and interpretation of the larger environment.

Each organization must manage a multitude of competing demands from its environment to ensure as stable as possible a supply of resources. Demands often conflict, however, and the response to current demands may influence an organization's ability to respond to other demands in the future. Goals and values become a key to understanding an organization's resolution to the problem of conflicting demands (Emery and Trist, 1965); they are invoked to legitimize the quest for a stable flow of resources. Two types of resources are desired: money and authority (Benson, 1975). Organizations desire authority in relation to particular domains, or areas in which they have the right and responsibility to carry out programs.

The University and Its Environment. The domains of the university are instruction (often referred to as the academic mission), research, and, to some extent, service. All educational institutions are interested in these three spheres, but research, scholarship, and intellectual leadership are the unique contributions of the large research-oriented university. The federal government became the major source of funds for university research projects following World War II, and federal support still comprises the largest percentage of research support monies in universities. Relationships with industry during this period have taken a backseat to relationships with federal programs (Pake, 1981).

Now, however, the environment is changing. Federal support for research is being cut back, threatening the domains of large research-oriented universities and creating increased competition for funds from alternative sources. While these are some institutions whose long histories of research contributions insure a relatively high status in the network of major research universities, the present increased competition has created pressures for most research-oriented universities to try to increase their prestige. They must seek new funding sources that will assist in improving their status, in attracting graduate students, and, eventually, in stablizing their flow of resources. Potential cooperative efforts must be viewed within this framework. Costs and benefits are calculated in terms of future, as well as present, resource acquisition.

In addition to demands from the environment for educational excellence and demands for research contributions, there are constant demands for application of the resources of the universities to problems existing in the larger social context. All of the demands from the environment cannot be met, and decision makers will attempt to respond positively to those which show the most potential for meeting present and future resource needs. Thus it is understandable that LAU desires cooperative relationships with organizations that will fund, or otherwise contribute to, research efforts by supporting research projects, graduate students, or distinguished faculty members. It follows that LAU will actively discourage cooperative efforts that are perceived as taking resources away from research or graduate education, or that contribute only to the domains of service or extension or low-level undergraduate education. In addition, LAU will attempt to maintain control over any cooperative relationships that are established.

The University as Environment. The department within the university also form a loosely coupled system with the larger environment of the institution. It is important that the impression of unity not be overestimated. All department chairpersons conducted their individual analyses of the relationship of this project to their domain and desired resource base. Mills was the project director; his department, nuclear engineering, became most closely associated with this project. The views of this department faculty, chairperson, and dean are most central in understanding the events described in this chapter. The department's apparent support of and adherence to the traditional values of university education and research conflicted with Mills's major involvement in a project associated with extension.

An extension instructional program would not necessarily be viewed negatively if the level of instruction was considered appropriate for supporting the domain of the department within the university. This program being designed for the TPC, however, was identified as "training," rather than education, by the department chairperson and training efforts do not involve regular faculty, as Mills and the dean, Bracier, explained.

The importance attached to this debate over education versus training is not peculiar to LAU, although many studies of education-industry cooperative arrangements have sidestepped this issue of education and training. It has been claimed that a clear distinction is not possible and muddies, rather than clarifies, the issues (Darkenwald, 1983; Lusterman, 1977; Peterfreund, 1976). The administrators in this project perceive that distinction as important in their enacted environments because it is connected to status in the university network.

For the mathematics department, this project did not diminish but enhanced the resources available for teaching and research. Appel was in a different position than was Mills. First, he was not the project director; the project required less of his time and was not identified with his department. Second, he desired consultant status on the project from the beginning; he is clear about his teaching and research responsibilities as a faculty member, is committed to that definition of his role, and was interested in supplemental income. Third, the TPC contract provided him with a programmer — a resource he badly needed in order to fulfill his primary roles within the university. It affected departmental domain positively when Appel published information about his emerging computer-assisted video instructional system in a professional journal. The fact that individual consulting in a training program had supported the system's development was largely irrelevant.

The service role traditionally has been accorded a low status in large universities. It is seen as subtracting from resources available for research and teaching, and, therefore, eventually diminishing a university's claim to resources which depend on intellectual and scholarly recognition (Johnson, 1974; Millett, 1973). Those departments and programs within the university which are dedicated primarily to service functions, such as the industrial extension service, are battling constantly to maintain their precarious resources, as Longstreet (industrial extension service) explained.

University continuing education, by its nature, is considered a source—or a channel—of environmental demands on the school of engineering. Its dedication to promoting the responsiveness of the university to these demands is in conflict with many administrators' desires to limit extension involvement. University continuing education personnel in this project attempted to avert problems by involving departmental administrators in the entire process of project negotiation and development. Conferences, signoff forms, and other mechanisms were created to facilitate clear communication. As the LAU-TPC project progressed, however, school of engineering administrators began to view it as a threat to their place in the research university network. Under those conditions the formal agreements ceased facilitating communication and were perceived more and more negatively. Regardless of whether one agrees with the rationales provided by the school of engineering administrators, the logic of their position is evident. A clear consequence of their position is the lengthy time frame projected for potential university involvement in Phase II, since faculty availability would be limited to summers.

The University Team and the Product. The members of the industry team, although disturbed by the university's scheduling demands, were far more upset by the inability of the university team to develop acceptable course outlines. The university team sincerely claimed that its proposal differed from regular university courses. They were comparing their product with standard university curricula and they knew that the modules presented to TPC did not have the breadth and depth required for university credit courses. The utility, however, compared the modules with the job task analyses they had conducted, and with the revised INPO guidelines. In that framework, the university's product had much more in common with traditional university courses than it did with the direct responsibilities of plant operators.

The professors on the team had no professional preparation for developing curricula. Their problems in this project were predictable according to the views of many authors. Schwab (1973), for example, describes five "bodies of experience," or areas of knowledge and understanding, that are necessary for successful curriculum development: subject matter, learners, milieus, teachers, and the curriculum-making process. The LAU professors possess the subject matter knowledge, but those members of the team most experienced in the other four areas (Longstreet and Curry) played only tangential roles.

In addition, the traditional domain of educational institutions is threatened by the burgeoning of in-house industrial education programs. One way of maintaining domain is to insist on authority of expertise, or control of the definition of education. The professors were concerned that the training program be done "right" and they produced course outlines that reflect the traditional disciplines. When challenged, they defended themselves on the grounds of professional expertise.

Mills was upset when he found that the annual reporting forms provided no legitimation of his service activities. The reporting forms reflect the underlying reward system of the university, which is intimately connected to the struggle for resources. Pfeffer and Salancik (1978) report on studies they and others have conducted on the determinants of the power of departments within large research-oriented universities, and of the power of individual faculty members within departments. They conclude that acquisition of outside grant and contract money, which enhances national scholarly reputations, determines the influence of individuals or departments within their organizations. However, as Dean Bracier explained, merely bringing in money is not enough. The grant must facilitate access to the scarce resources of research funding and graduate students; it must enhance the domain of the organization.

Theorists appear to agree that some level of trust is necessary for successful cooperative efforts and that it is important to develop interpersonal relationships between the industry and the university personnel over a fairly lengthy period of time (Cullitan, 1982; Prager and Omenn, 1980). In the LAU-TPC project there was minimal communication between the teams, other than that between the two liaison persons. The professors' personal social networks are composed predominantly of others from the academic world. Mills, new to the academic world and largely isolated within his department, was unable to mediate effectively.

Mistrust of the utility was enhanced by prior negative relationships with other utilities and by the specific objectives of this project: training nuclear power plant operators. It is public knowledge that inadequate training appears to have contributed to the Three Mile Island accident (Rogovin and Frampton, 1980). The professors wanted to exploit an opportunity to assist in the prevention of any similar event. They appeared to believe that education was a key, and the more education, the better. This is not an unusual viewpoint (Gannella and Zeleznik, 1983). It is quite possible that they overemphasized the role of education in addressing an issue that involves many additional factors, such as control room design, instrumentation, and appropriate simulation practice (Rogovin and Frampton, 1980).

The Utility and Its Environment. The diminishing level of federal support for university research affects industry, one of the primary consumers of the products of such efforts (knowledge and university program graduates). As universities turn to industry to support their research programs, industrial decision makers also must evaluate competing budgetary demands and protect their resource bases. Industries as well as universities are concerned about the nature of the tradeoffs and compromises necessary for any successful cooperative arrangement; there is an extensive literature about the emerging "academic-industrial complex" (Cullitan, 1982). Universities are wary of loss of intellectual independence and displacement of the goals of liberal university education in favor of more narrow occupational preparation. Industry is concerned about its accountability to shareholders and the difficulties of evaluating potential relationships when no clearcut product can be specified in advance (Bach and Thornton, 1983).

One major pressure in the utility's environment that precipitated this relationship was the act of a federal regulatory agency, the NRC. In order to protect its future domain (assuring continued licensing), the utility had to respond to the NRC's 1980 proposal for credential requirements for nuclear plant operators, and it turned to the university for assistance. Therefore, the decisions made by utility personnel cannot be understood solely on the basis of the extent to which they approved or disapproved of the course content developed by the university team. As long as their environment included a potential mandate for a relationship with a university, their choices were limited. While the project was being conducted, however, the environment was changing. INPO was developing as the industry's response to the findings of the Three Mile Island investigations, and INPO guidelines were being revised constantly. The NRC's original letter suggesting the need for university credit was never retracted, but neither was it promoted. The steps in the rule making procedure are not yet completed. INPO's recommended course outlines paralleled the job task analysis more closely than had previous guidelines, implying that the legal standards would be lower than originally anticipated. Although the possibility remains that degrees may be required in the future for shift supervisors, it became clear that the relationship between TPC and LAU could be terminated at the end of Phase I without any immediate loss of domain for the utility.

The pressure for training program improvement has not abated, however. TPC was vulnerable as long as it depended on LAU as its primary source of educational expertise. Therefore, it is understandable that the company began hiring continuing educators while also initiating relationships with local community colleges and universities. All of these actions futher reduced TPC's dependency on its relationship with LAU.

TPC was changing internally as well. Morton (vice-president) initiated the project, including Frankel (training director) in the early negotiations. Hirsch (supervisor, training development) joined the project as the proposal for Phase I was being developed and became the main liaison with LAU. Frankel left for a year, Morton was transferred and Davis becamse vice-president for nuclear operations. It is difficult to assess the impact of these personnel changes, but they certainly made it difficult to establish long-term interpersonal relationships between the teams of the two organizations. They also raise the possibility that expectations about the product may have changed between the original meeting at LAU and the final report review.

Much has been written about the basically different goal structures and values in industrial and educational organizations leading to difficulties in establishing and maintaining cooperative relationships (Pake, 1981; Tatel and Guthrie, 1983). The decision made by TPC administrators during this collaborative effort may be partially understood as a result of these factors. They were concerned with maintaining the production of electric power at a reasonable cost to consumers and providing a profit for their shareholders. Therefore, an educational program requiring millions of dollars for development and long hours of classroom study for power plant operators is far from their ideal.

Part Three: Principles for Cooperative Curriculum Projects

Hopefully, this case study serves as a kind of multifaceted model from which we may extract some guidance for developing future cooperative projects. It is not intended as a means of allocating praise or fault for a task done well or poorly, but as an example which may assist our efforts in the future.

We must try to be realistic as we plan cooperative efforts between large research-oriented universities and industries. Schools of engineering in major American universities probably will not become involved in cooperative projects simply for the money. The competition for the research domain is too fierce. The service component of such schools is not going to increase in the near future. Indeed, it will probably continue to be on the endangered list. Professors will have great difficulty understanding, without assistance, how to design applied industrial training programs without simply slicing content out of their broadly conceptualized, traditional university courses.

Acceptance of these caveats leads to some principles that may facilitate cooperative efforts in the future.

1. Although this project involves nuclear power plants, the nuclear engineer could have played only a technical role, similar to that of the mathematics and chemistry professors. There are units in universities responsible for furthering educational program development, such as some adult and continuing education departments. Their faculty often have the backgrounds to engage collaboratively and productively with industry. *These faculty should direct such projects, rather than serve in tangential roles.*

2. It would be extremely difficult for a nuclear engineer to engage in nuclear reactor research in the course of this project. Continuing educators, on the other hand, would find many opportunities for inquiry. Cooperative programming projects can be conceptualized creatively to include research opportunities for a project director from the continuing or adult education department, further addressing the realities of contemporary university survival. *Program development does not preclude research when the process or the product is the focus of inquiry.*

3. The cost-benefit calculations of the school of engineering administrators in this project were based on a set of commonly held values and assumptions that are consistently applied to establish priorities and make decisions. Potential project administrators should realistically assess organizational ideology, priorities, and values and *seriously question appointing faculty to major roles, such as project director, when such involvement could create or intensify conflict between faculty members and their colleagues.* The project itself, as well as the faculty member, may suffer from lack of organizational support.

4. The relationship with a single individual, Morton, was deemed crucial for this project's continuation. His reassignment, however, was not unusual. In addition, there was minimal contact between the university team and industry personnel either within or outside of the project. *A broad base of relationships should be established between the cooperating organizations, and multiple opportunities for social as well as professional interaction should be provided.*

5. All of the members of the industry team learned about the university the hard way. They were forced to respond to unexpected conditions and attitudes, and to derive some explanation of the university as an organization. The university team, likewise, learned about industry as they attempted collaboration. The teams reached what Frankel described as an impasse. However, even a cursory examination of the literature reveals that the patterns exhibited by both organizations are not unique. It is possible that some prior literature review and reflection may have facilitated this project. Future project teams should be encouraged to reflect upon their own and each other's culture, and to educate each other about particular assumptions, values, or goal orientations that may otherwise hinder communication. *They should be encouraged to share broad professional orientations as well as knowledge specific to the project at hand.*

6. Team members knowledgeable about the learners, milieus, teachers, curriculum development process, and subject matter must develop a partnership in which they learn from each other in order to create something new and appropriate. We must not assume that subject matter experts are skilled in curriculum development. This type of cross-disciplinary teamwork is unusual in the university; *successful projects may require training in cooperative teamwork as well as in curriculum development.* Not all university professors desire involvement in a project that may break with some of the traditions of their disciplines. *Team members should be chosen carefully on the basis of their willingness to participate in this kind of partnership as well as on the basis of their technical expertise.*

Cooperative projects entail a process of negotiated exchange. Each organization calculates what it needs and desires from the other as well as what it is willing to offer. In this case study each group appears to have desired control rather than mutual exchange. The resultant lack of mutual satisfaction may be understood as a lack of consensus on the effects of environmental forces and on the choice of criteria for evaluating possible responses.

It is not simple to juggle the organization's place in its primary professional network, its loosely coupled connections to other professional organizations and networks, and its dynamic internal networks. That is the challenge that confronts us, however, as we continue learning how to develop successful linkages between universities and industries.

References

Bach, M. L., and Thornton, R. "Academic-Industrial Partnerships in Biomedical Research: Inevitability and Desirability." *Educational Record,* 1983, *64* (2), 26-32.

Benson, K. J. "The Interorganizational Network as a Political Economy." *Administrative Science Quarterly,* 1975, *20,* 229-249.

Cullitan, B. J. "The Academic-Industrial Complex." *Science,* May 28, 1982, *216,* 960–962.
Darkenwald, G. G. "Perspectives of Business and Industry on Cooperative Programming with Educational Institutions." *Adult Education Quarterly,* 1983, *33* (4), 230–243.
Deuton, H. R., director, Office of Nuclear Reactor Regulation, Nuclear Regulatory Commission. Memo to power reactor applicant licensees. Washington, D.C., March 1980.
Emery, R. E., and Trist, E. L. "The Causal Texture of Organizational Environments." *Human Relations,* 1965, *18,* 21–32.
Gannella, J. S., and Zeleznik, C. "Strengthening the Relations Between Professional Education and Performance." In S. Grabowski (Ed.), *Strengthening Connections Between Education and Performance.* New Directions for Continuing Education, no. 18. San Francisco: Jossey-Bass, 1983.
Johnson, E. L. "The Internal Image." In *National Conference on Public Service and Extension in Institutions of Higher Education Conference Proceedings.* University of Georgia, Center for Continuing Education, Athens, Ga., 1974.
Litwak, E., with Rothman, J. "Towards the Theory and Practice of Coordinating Between Formal Organizations." In W. R. Rosengren and M. Lefton (Eds.), *Organizations and Clients: Essays in the Sociology of Service.* Columbus, Ohio: Merrill, 1970.
Lusterman, S. *Education in Industry.* New York: The Conference Board, 1977.
Millett, J. D. "Similarities and Differences Among Universities of the United States." In J. A. Perkins (Ed.), *The University as an Organization.* New York: McGraw-Hill, 1973.
Pake, G. E. "Industry-University Interactions." *Physics Today,* January 1981, *34,* 44–48.
Peterfreund, S. "Education in Industry—Today and in the Future." *Training and Development Journal,* May 1976, *30,* 30–40.
Pfeffer, J., and Salancik, G. R. *The External Control of Organizations: A Resource Dependence Perspective.* New York: Harper & Row, 1978.
Prager, D. J., and Omenn, G. S. "Research, Innovation and University-Industry Linkages." *Science,* 1980, *207,* 379–384.
Rogovin, M., and Frampton, G. T., Jr. *Three Mile Island: A Report to the Commissioners and to the Public.* Washington, D.C.: Nuclear Regulatory Commission Special Inquiry Group Report, 1980.
Schwab, J. J. "The Practical 3: Translation into Curriculum." *School Review,* 1973, *81,* 501–522.
Tatel, D. S., and Guthrie, R. C. "The Legal Ins and Outs of University-Industry Collaboration." *Educational Record,* 1983, *64* (2), 19–25.
Yuchtman, E., and Seashore, S. E. "A System Resource Approach to Organizational Effectiveness." *American Sociological Review,* 1967, *32,* 891–903.

Arlene Fingeret is assistant professor of adult and community college education at North Carolina State University, Raleigh, North Carolina. Previously she was assistant professor at the College of Public and Community Service, University of Massachusetts at Boston.

*Poorly handled collaborations can undermine a
promising continuing education enterprise.*

The Consequences of Mismanaged Interagency Collaborations

Thomas Valentine

From the day it opened its doors, the Crawford City Adult Education Center seemed destined to succeed. The center, which was operated by Sandoe County Community College, had been established through the joint initiative of a host of powerful organizations, whose representatives now served on its advisory committee. These organizations included the State Department of Education's Special Branch for Adult Education, the Sandoe County Manpower Commission, the Crawford Board of Education, the Crawford Coalition for Urban Renewal, the Office of the Mayor of Crawford, Crofton-Roberts Pharmaceutical Corporation, and Central State University. The center housed a full range of continuing education programs designed to meet the needs of the undereducated and underemployed residents of the greater Crawford area; offered services included literacy tutoring, adult basic education for the handicapped, regular adult basic education, adult secondary education, English as a second language, career exploration and assessment, vocational training, and a comprehensive employment counseling and placement service. The center's budget was large

The locale and organizations discussed in this chapter in reality bear different names.

and diversified, with operating funds supplied by five distinct governmental agencies. Within one year, the center had outgrown its 12,000 square-foot headquarters facility, and had opened an extension site with an additional 3,000 square feet of instructional space.

By the end of its fourth year of operation, however, the Crawford City Adult Education Center was very nearly defunct. Advisory committee meetings were spiritless and poorly attended, and members offered little but nodding sympathy. Only two programs had survived, a part-time General Educational Development (GED) program and a job placement service. Operating monies, drawn from two governmental agencies, were so scarce that the center found itself unable to meet the rent on the single remaining site.

The question, of course, is why. How did a promising continuing education enterprise, in the space of a few years, go from being an exemplar of success to the epitome of failure? The director of the center points to a shift in the political *zeitgeist* and an accompanying change in funding priorities. An embittered and displaced staff points to poor leadership and ineffective funding strategies on the part of the director. This writer, however, suggests that the failure of the Crawford Center can be explained, to a significant extent, by a history of mismanaged, misbegotten, and never-begotten attempts at interagency collaboration.

The central message of this chapter is that collaborations can and do cut both ways, and that considerable administrative foresight and effort are required to make them pay off. Too often, the anticipated benefits are so attractive that they blind the unwary administrator to the potential hazards of collaboration, hazards which tend to be insidious and recognizable only when substantial administrative energy is required simply to recapture an agency's original position in the larger environment. In effect, this chapter might best be viewed as a companion piece to Beder's opening chapter. The latter takes an optimistic stance and provides readers with an opportunity to learn from successful instances of interagency collaboration. The present chapter examines the sources, dynamics, and consequences of unsuccessful collaborations.

Key Concepts

The concepts to be used in the following discussion have been explicated in Beder's opening chapter. Before examining the failure of the Crawford Center, however, it seems desirable to briefly recapitulate two of these concepts, namely interagency linkages and interagency collaboration.

Interagency linkages are the contact points between agencies, the channels through which resources flow from one organization to another. Linkages, in and of themselves, are neither good nor bad because there is nothing inherent in the concept "linkage" which denotes an exchange, as opposed to a surrendering, of program resources. Sometimes such surrenderings, or one-way resource flows, can be highly desirable from an administrative viewpoint, depending on your position in respect to that flow. When a teacher in Program A repeatedly "loans" scarce instructional materials to an unreciprocating teacher in Program B, a linkage has been implemented which, if known, would be satisfactory to the administrator of Program B, but considerably less so to the administrator in Program A. This example points to another characteristic of interagency linkages: They can exist and flourish without administrative knowledge, initiative, or control.

Interagency collaboration, in the somewhat restricted sense used in this discussion, denotes a goal-oriented exchange or co-allocation of resources engineered and implemented by the administrators of two or more agencies. In essence, collaboration consists of the intentional formation and use of linkages to achieve an agency's goals. As the initial definition implies, collaborations occur in one of two modes.

In the first mode, exchange collaborations, each agency separately continues to pursue its own goals, but the functioning of each is augmented by the acquisition of needed resources through the relinquishing of some other resources. In the ideal situation, an administrator in an agency possessing Resource A (for example, physical space) but in need of Resource B (for example, counseling services) will engineer an exchange with the administrator of a second agency possessing Resource B but in need of Resource A. In this example, the first administrator has relinquished space in order to extend services offered by the agency; the second administrator has exchanged staff hours and expertise for the opportunity to reach more clients and extend the agency's territorial domain. Neither administrator has had to relinquish money; both have had to relinquish some degree of control. It should be noted that even what Beder calls a donor-receiver relationship (in Chapter One of this volume) is a type of exchange collaboration. If a corporate foundation awards operating funds to a continuing education agency, it is relinquishing one resource (money) in exchange for image, tax benefits, and the furtherance of a program which is in philosophical accord with the foundation's mission.

In the second mode, *cosponsored collaborations,* two or more agencies agree to contribute different available resources toward the accomplishment of a common provisional goal which no one agency could have achieved—or could have achieved as cost-effectively—

working independently. For instance, if a legal services clinic unites with a continuing education agency to co-sponsor a brief course in divorce law on the premises of the latter, the common goal (the offering of a novel service to appropriate clients) is attained through the strategic combination of resources, which, rather than flow from one agency to another, flow to a *pro tempore* activity which, in respect to domain and control, neither agency can claim as its own. Such an arrangement is possible only when two agencies have both compatible goals and complementary resource availability. The legal services clinic, by contributing staff and expertise, is able to advance its mission to disseminate legal information to the public. The continuing education agency, by contributing learners and instructional space, is able to advance its mission to provide varied and relevant educational services to its clientele.

Failure of the Crawford Education Center

There was no single cause for the failure of the Crawford Center. Neither was that failure in any way dramatic: There was no portentous moment when the fate of the center hung in the balance, no visible denouement, no climax. With the benefit of hindsight, it is possible to recognize a turning point midway through the second year of operation, but it is doubtful that anyone involved noticed it at the time. Rather, the failure of the Crawford Center was the inevitable outcome of a history comprised of many small failures and too few successes. This account will describe only the failures, and of those, only those which involved, or should have involved, some form of interagency collaboration.

Crawford City covers five square miles, has a population of fifty thousand, and is located in the northeastern United States. The city was founded in the late seventeenth century on the north bank of the Sandoe River, and by the middle of the nineteenth century it was a booming mill town located at the nexus of a growing water, rail, and highway transportation network. By the middle of the twentieth century, it was ugly, impoverished, and in an advanced state of urban decay.

The last of the old mills closed in 1956. The large military base on the outskirts of the city was downgraded to a small reserve installation in 1962, leaving behind a legacy of brothels and seedy bars. By the early seventies, the city consisted of a core of substandard housing and failing retail businesses surrounded by a few stable but ethnically entrenched neighborhoods populated by southern European immigrants and their descendents. The campuses of Central State University flanked the city, literally and figuratively on the right sides of the two railroad tracks. The only remaining major industry was Crofton-Roberts Pharmaceutical Corporation, whose headquarters abutted the oldest university campus, and whose subsidiary manufacturing plants were scattered throughout the greater Crawford area.

In 1975, Crawford City began to revive when, largely in response to Croften-Roberts's threat to locate its proposed new international headquarters in the suburbs, the city developed a master plan for urban renewal. Much of Crawford's substandard housing was summarily demolished and replaced, not with more desirable low income housing, but with modern office buildings surrounded by acres of lawn. The small public hospital quadrupled in size as it became a teaching hospital for the university's medical school. The Main Street business district was given a facelift, the brothels and bars giving way to bookstores, boutiques, and restaurants. The way in which one viewed Crawford's urban renewal, however, was largely a function of where one was located on the have-have not continuum.

For most of the power elites, it was considered an unparalleled triumph. Crawford's mayor experienced landslide victories in election after election and, as his political base steadily increased, a state senatorship appeared to be well within his grasp. Croften-Roberts was granted huge tax breaks for remaining in the city. Through the creation of a nonprofit property development corporation, the pharmaceutical company was systematically purchasing and developing (read "leveling") the less desirable areas of the inner-city. Croften-Roberts's power in the city was considerably augmented by the formation of a second nonprofit organization in collaboration with the mayor's office; this organization, the Crawford Coalition for Urban Renewal, was charged with the overall implementation of the master plan. Central State University benefitted from the changes indirectly by the city's improving reputation among alumni and potential students, and directly by the low rent charged by the property development corporation for university-affiliated art and theater facilities in the inner city.

The poor, largely minority population of inner city Crawford, however, was losing much and gaining little through the urban renewal efforts. Homes were being destroyed and, since alternative housing was not being provided, many residents were being effectively driven out of the city in which they had been born. Neighborhoods which were not destroyed were being invaded by the middle class; renovations increased property values, and increased property values resulted in increased rents which the poor could no longer afford. Community groups sprang up, and community newspapers began to level charges at the mayor, at the Coalition, and at Crofton-Roberts that the bricks-and-mortar development efforts were proceeding without any parallel effort to develop the city's human resources. New jobs were being created, but the people who needed them most lacked the skills to gain and keep employment.

Before the creation of the Crawford Adult Education Center, educational opportunities for undereducated and underemployed adults were virtually nonexistent. The Board of Education's new superintendent was devoting all of her energy to the restructuring of the much-criticized K-12 system, and had little interest in resurrecting continuing education—the program had been inoperative for over two years as a result of poor management, and ultimately, the forced resignation of its acting director. The State Department of Education was willing to fund any viable Adult Basic Education/General Education Development (ABE/GED) program operating in Crawford; they were, however, unable to find such a program, and were annoyed at the large number of potential learners going unserved. Sandoe County College offered programs which might appeal to Crawford residents, but all were located at its suburban campus seven miles outside the city. The Dean of Community Extension had been admonished by the college president for neglecting a large population of potential fund-generating students. Central State University had been criticized for its implicit entrenchment policies, and for a lack of any meaningful community participation.

In short, the time was right for a major continuing education effort in Crawford City. The power elites were being subjected to annoying, but not particularly threatening, pressure to develop Crawford's human capital, something they were willing to do if the rest of the renewal plan could proceed on schedule. The absence of continuing education in the city and the pool of available learners boded well for programs that operate on an enrollment economy. In fact, all of the key pieces were ready and waiting except one: money. The state department of education was eager to supply operating funds for academic programming, but the level of funding was too low to institute a program sizable enough and with broad enough purpose to assuage the growing bitterness in the community. Any continuing education enterprise which could find someone to pick up the initial tab could call Crawford its own.

Failure Number One: Misleading the Advisory Committee. It was the president of the Coalition for Urban Renewal who discovered the missing piece: With the fiscal year nearly three-quarters over, the Sandoe County Manpower Commission found itself with an embarrassing amount of unspent funds. The president knew the value of this information, and immediately contacted his long-time friend, the Dean of Community Extension at Sandoe County Community College. Together they mapped out a plan which would allow the dean to increase considerably his budget and domain by moving into Crawford and setting up a comprehensive continuing education center fueled by Manpower Commission dollars, with additional support from the state. A series of subsequent meetings were held with the director of the commission, who was enthusiastically receptive to a plan which would allow her to utilize her surplus budget to create, through the college, an innovative program which would centralize her fragmented manpower development efforts.

Were the arrangements made public at this time, the foregoing account would be nothing less than a stellar example of cosponsorship collaboration. Each of the three organizations had advanced its individual goals through the contribution of available resources toward the accomplishment of a common goal, in this case the establishment of a novel program. The Manpower Training Commission had contributed funds in order to accomplish, through the college, the education and training of the underemployed. The coalition had furthered the cause of urban renewal (and public relations) through the contribution of information and administrative effort. The college had fulfilled its mandate to provide community education by contributing legitimacy (image) and educational expertise.

The arrangements, however, were not made public at this time. Both the dean and the coalition's president believed that if the plan were to succeed they would need the support of the other major organizations who had a stake in Crawford's future. Therefore, after the arrangements were finalized, and only after the arrangements were finalized, the president convened a meeting of representatives from all the organizations concerned. To all appearances, the meeting took the form of a problem-solving forum focusing on the question, "Given that Crawford City is in dire need of continuing education, what should we do?" The negotiations which had already been concluded were not discussed, however, and most of the participants, powerful members of politically powerful organizations, came away eager to do their part in a burgeoning, but not yet fully formed, enterprise. But they came away with something else, something which the dean and the coalition's president had failed to foresee: They came away with a sense of *ownership*.

Two weeks later, when the college announced its plan to open the Crawford Center under the directorship of a full-time college staff member, the same participants who had attended the forum were asked to serve on the advisory committee. They enthusiastically accepted, and this initial support did much to get the center off to a booming start. Their sense of ownership, however, now heightened by membership on an advisory committee whose role was never clearly defined, soon became a bit too earnest for the college's liking.

The representative from Central State University drew up a master plan for the development of the center, a plan which clearly depicted the center as a cosponsorship collaboration belonging, in part, to each of the "founding" organizations, with the college playing a central, but by no means dominant, role. The plan was neither rejected nor implemented; it was graciously received and nonchalantly shelved.

Then the Board of Education approached the dean with a full-blown plan to install the board's new adult basic/secondary education program in the center. Moreover, the plan had the whole-hearted support of the State Department of Education and of the mayor's office. The college was not happy with the plan, in that they had a similar program of their own ready to move into the center from their suburban campus. It was impossible, however, to refuse the offer without alienating three members of the advisory committee and thus shattering the myth of shared ownership. Ultimately, the college acquiesced to the board's plan, but, in an effort to maintain control of the center, they did so with the understanding that the college would continue to pay the total rent on the facility. This arrangement, as will be described in a subsequent section, had some rather far-reaching consequences.

By this point in the narrative, the lack of consensus on the nature of the existing collaboration is readily apparent. The college clearly saw the relationship as an exchange collaboration with the advisory committee, with the committee members contributing political support, information, and, in some cases, funds in exchange for the prestige they could gain from the association with a center belonging to the college. The more active committee members, however, viewed the center as the product of cosponsorship collaboration, in which the resources they were contributing were flowing not to the college, but to a jointly created entity which was, at least in part, under their control.

In order to perpetuate the myth of cosponsorship without surrendering the control of the center, the college incurred additional costs. By allowing the board program, and eventually several other minor programs, to operate in the center rent free, the college paid for the collaboration by relinquishing space and ultimately potential learners for their own similar program (and the funds such learners generate) in exchange for continued political support.

The issue of ownership of the center was never openly resolved, and, as a result, controversies related to domain and control, though usually subdued and short-lived, periodically surfaced. The cumulative effect of these controversies was the alienation of the members of the advisory committee as they slowly came to realize just who was running, and who had always been running, the center. Sensing the waning of enthusiasm, and in some cases support, the college became increasingly more guarded about the agendas for advisory committee meetings. Meetings degenerated into passive affairs during which the college would discuss only the center's successes—never its failures or problems—and the ever-present need for more operating monies. Attendance at the meetings fell off, and it was not unusual for members to send representatives in their stead.

In respect to resource flow, the college continued to contribute rent-free space and learners to the programs sponsored by advisory committee members, and continued to devote administrative time and effort to dealing with the advisory committee. In return, the college received only guarded and, at times, halfhearted support.

Failure Number Two: Alienating the United Hispanic Alliance. The center had been open for about four months when the director was approached by the coalition's president with a suggestion. Several community leaders had noticed that Crawford's Hispanic population was underrepresented among the center's clientele, and that something had to be done to increase the involvement of this politically vocal group.

The director decided that the easiest way to stem the growing criticism was to enter into some kind of cooperative relationship with the United Hispanic Alliance, a small but politically active social and educational program on the other side of the city. He approached the alliance's president, not with a mutually beneficial plan for the establishment of interagency linkages, but with a blanket offer: "If there is anything we can do for your clients, let me know." He was contacted that same week with a request. The alliance had heard of the center's large career program, and was wondering if some of their clients might participate. When the director said they would be welcome, the president of the alliance said they would be over the following week.

If the center's career program was large, it was large in terms of the number of participants, not in terms of staff. The program, which was staffed by two professionals and three aides, was in many respects a logistical nightmare. Each Monday the Manpower Commission referred an average of sixty new participants to a program which was designed to run for two full weeks. This necessitated having two staggered groups, totalling more than one hundred participants, moving through a rigid schedule of orientation, achievement testing, aptitude testing, audiovisual presentations, assorted career-oriented workshops, and individual career counseling.

Midway through Wednesday morning, fifteen Hispanic clients turned up at the center to participate in the program. None of the program staff spoke Spanish; few of the Hispanic clients could speak, understand, read, or write English with anything approaching fluency. Moreover, the director, who was not in the building when the group arrived, had neglected to inform his staff about his already-accepted invitation to the alliance. After fragmented conversation with the guests and two telephone calls to the alliance, the program's coordinator decided to integrate the group into the activities scheduled for the afternoon.

The activities scheduled for the afternoon, however, were achievement tests in reading and writing. The Hispanic participants could not understand the oral directions, let alone the tests themselves, and the test administrator found himself in the rather farcical position of repeating the test directions ever more slowly and ever more loudly, in the best "ugly American" tradition. The resulting chaos disrupted the session, delayed the schedule, and satisfied no one, least of all the frustrated Hispanic clients who returned to the alliance program early in the afternoon.

All of the mistakes involved in this attempted collaboration can be traced to the omission of a key step in any collaborative venture: planning. The director approached the alliance without any semblance of strategy, with perhaps a vague notion of exchanging existing services for increased political support, but with the determination to form *some* kind of cooperative relationship. By agreeing to the request of the alliance's president, he revealed a lack of understanding of his own resources and failed to clarify the needs of the alliance; consequently, he offered to expend an acutely scarce resource, and, given the unforeseen (yet quite foreseeable) language barrier, he tacitly promised to deliver what his program did not possess: bilingual career education. In addition to the lack of an initial plan for collaboration, the director failed to institute even the most rudimentary procedures for implementing the collaboration, as evidenced by the unexpected arrival of alliance clients. Not only did he fail to set a schedule for the visit, but he failed to notify his staff that visitors were coming. Finally, owing to the embarrassing nature of the incident, he neglected to follow up the failed attempt with a more reasonable plan for collaboration, such as the loan of bilingual audiovisual materials to the alliance program. In the final analysis, the attempted collaboration with the United Hispanic

Alliance resulted in a decrease in the center's community image among Crawford's Hispanic population, a potental political foe in the alliance's president, an afternoon of program disruption, and frustration and alienation on the part of the instructional staff. The political support the director had sought was not forthcoming.

Failure Number Three: Competing with the Crawford Board of Education. The center had been open for six months when the Board of Education's new adult basic/secondary education (ABSE) program opened for business. Partially because space in the center was already at a premium, and partially because the board program was a rent-free—and somewhat unwelcome—guest program in the college's center, the director assigned it to what he considered to be an undesirable and nearly unusable location: the heavily-trafficked 400 square feet of open space immediately inside the main doors.

The coordinator of the board program was delighted. The location *was* useless for instructional purposes, but it would be difficult to imagine a better location to conduct continuous informal recruitment. A large and ever-changing population of eligible learners, participants of other center programs, walked within yards of the coordinator's desk several times a day; further, since the center had no centralized intake and information counseling, walk-ins tended to approach her desk to find out what the center could offer them. Within four months, the board's instructional sites, scattered throughout the public schools of Crawford, were operating at full capacity.

Meanwhile, the college proceeded with its plan to establish its own ABSE program in Crawford. The college program came to the center one month after the board program, and was allocated four large, quiet classrooms in the newly opened extension site a quarter of a mile away from the main building. Since its inception, the program had relied on the referral of learners receiving stipends from the Manpower Commission. When the stipends were discontinued one year after the program moved to Crawford, the college was put in the unfamiliar position of having to recruit unsubsidized learners.

If there was any true collaboration between the college and the board, it existed only on the highest administrative levels, and took the form of a space-for-support exchange linkage. The notion of collaboration never filtered down to the coordinators of the two ABSE programs. In reality, the nearly identical nature of the two programs precluded any useful resource transfer. Both programs offered essentially the same services to the same potential learners, resided in the same domain, and drew their funds, in part, from the same funding source. Resource scarcities and resource availabilities in the two programs were not complementary, but identical. The resultant situation was a classic example of duplication of services, and when such a situation occurs, competition is almost inevitable. The more resources one program garners, the less that are available to the other. Unless some form of domain consensus is achieved, and in this case it was never even discussed, each program will continue to seek growth at the expense of its rival. Although, for the most part, open hostility was avoided, tension between the programs steadily increased. Despite its central location, the board program was never considered to be, and was never treated as, an integral part of the center. Press releases for the center went out on college letterhead, and the board program was never mentioned. When public relations ceremonies were held, the podium was draped with the college's banner, and the board program administrators were not asked to participate—in fact, the staff of the program received mailed invitations to the ceremony as if they were outsiders.

Although the coordinator of the board program fully realized that she was not welcome in the center and had little to say about its overall operation, she did not sever ties. She found it well worth tolerating the affronts and slights of the college so long as she could maintain her excellent operating base. The situation, by the end of the second year, had devolved into a user relationship—in spirit, but not in appearance, the antithesis of collaboration. She felt little allegiance to the center as an organization, and even less to the director and dean. The board program continued to occupy space in the center, continued to avail itself of sundry support services which the college supplied (copier, audio-visual equipment, etc.), and continued to recruit students from the broader center population. Meanwhile, the board coordinator repeatedly complained to her superintendent about the college's constant affronts, thus effectively obviating any political support which the board might have offered to the college.

The director of the center considered the board program to be not a threat but an annoyance, something which he could not control and which he, therefore, wished would go away. In keeping with the haphazard way in which he managed all collaborations, he failed to monitor the consequences of the collaboration with the board. In fact, he was not in a position to do so; since the new extension site contained a larger and more comfortable office than anything the main center had to offer, he had moved himself out of the arena of action. As a result, he failed to notice the formation of a linkage of which he would never have approved: College-sponsored programs in the center began referring clients in need of a high school credential not to the college ABSE program, which was located at the extension site, but to the board program, which was right in the heart of the center. Consequently, the board program was constantly overenrolled, while the college's program was chronically underenrolled. Ironically, when the board's waiting list grew cumbersome, they placed learners temporarily in the college program. These students were "loans," however, rather than true referrals.

The attempted collaboration with the board represents a dismal failure in respect to resource exchange. The college surrendered rent-free space, support services, recruitment opportunities, and active referrals, all in a vain attempt to garner political support and prolong the myth of cosponsorship. In return it received essentially nothing. Toward the end of the fourth year, when the center operations had dwindled to the point where there was little incentive for the board program to remain, the college requested that the board begin paying a share of the rent. The board refused, opting instead to open its own large learning center in downtown Crawford. The college's ABSE program lost the majority of its funding, and was reduced to a part-time GED program with a staff of one.

Failure Number Four. Antagonizing the University Mental Health Services Program. Central State University's Mental Health Services Program, which was designed to serve the nonstudent population in the greater Crawford area, offered clinical adult basic education programming for the emotionally and psychologically handicapped. Each participant was given intensive individualized instruction that was designed in light of carefully prepared and constantly updated psychological, social, and academic profiles. Prior to the establishment of the Crawford Center, all instruction took place on a university campus some three miles from the central city. When the center opened, the professor who coordinated the program, cognizant of the fact that the university was in on the collaboration, saw the opportunity for community outreach. Through the Coalition for Urban Renewal, he requested instructional space.

The director of the center was especially unhappy about this request, not only because he had little use for autonomous guest programs, but also because there was longstanding personal animosity between the professor and himself. Yet, against his inclinations, and, once more, to foster the myth of cosponsorship, the director allocated rent-free but limited use of classroom space to the clinical ABE program. Selective forgetting being what it is, it is not surprising that the director neglected to inform his staff of the new arrangement, and the instructor from the clinical ABE program arrived to find a large English-as-a-second-language class occupying the promised space. Instruction had to take place in the limited privacy offered by the corner of an occupied classroom, a setting absolutely at odds with the approach used by the clinical ABE program, in which unconstrained dialogue is essential.

Eventually the space scheduling issue was resolved, but the animosity between the two administrators showed no signs of abating. In fact, the director found a new outlet for his feelings. The clinical ABE program was funded primarily by the State Department of Education, which provided partial funding for the college's ABSE program. The director began denigrating the clinical program, arguing that the cost per contact hour was five times what it was in his own program, and that it was of questionable wisdom to devote so much money to so few learners. These comments were passed in several quarters, eventually reaching the funding source, and ultimately coming to the attention of the professor coordinating the program. The professor continued to use the classroom space, but became the avowed enemy of the director, seldom missing an opportunity to malign the center and the way it was being managed. He did, however, cement ties with the board program, ties which continue to the present day. Once again, the director saw the collaboration as a space-for-support exchange linkage. Once again, he failed to obtain the support.

Failure Number Five: Overdependence on the Manpower Commission. When the collaboration between the college and the Manpower Commission was begun, it appeared to be a perfect marriage, in that the two agencies had compatible goals and complementary resource availabilities. The overarching goal of the commission was to educate the unemployed and underemployed so that they would be able to join the work force; the commission had the funds to do the job, but lacked a sufficient number of qualified educational providers. Further, their operation suffered from fragmentation and duplication of services caused by scattered providers. The college's extension division was charged with offering a variety of educational services to the broader, noncollegiate community, but lacked the funds to carry out this mandate. The initial collaboration was accurately viewed as an exchange linkage, in which the college contributed expertise and image in exchange for financial and political support, domain expansion, and learner referrals.

By the end of the first year, the commission was supporting five programs in the center through direct funding and through referral of stipended learners: the college ABSE program, the career program, a secretarial training program, an electronics training program, and a job placement program. The fact that the commission was paying the full rent on the center buildings, contributing 90 percent of the college's staff salaries at the center, and referring virtually all of the center's learners (with the exception of those in the guest programs) put the college in a rather precarious position in respect to autonomy and control. Fortunately, this issue did not arise during the first two years of operation.

Unfortunately, it arose with a vengeance in the beginning of the third year. For some time the Manpower Commission had been accused of wasteful inefficiency, and suddenly legislators were prepared to act on those accusations. Faced with imminent extinction, the commission began to scrutinize the programs they were funding solely in light of the cost per job placement. Since legislators were interested in results, and only in results, such considerations as the number and types of learners served and the diversity of offerings became unimportant and unaffordable luxuries.

The programs in the center had been designed so that, ideally, a student of quite low ability could experience a total career development process. Starting with the state-funded literacy tutorial program, a student could then successively enter a chain of commission-funded programs: first, the ABSE program, then the career program, next a vocational training program, and finally the job placement program. Compiled statistics, cold and simple, demonstrated the rather obvious fact that it was considerably cheaper to place highly qualified people than those in need of the full range of offerings. In fact, there was little financial justification for continuing the lower level programs when Crawford's ever-rising unemployment rate created a pool of experienced, academically proficient, but temporarily unemployed work seekers who could directly enter the job placement program.

In the course of the following six months, the commission ceased the funding of the ABSE program, dismantled the career program, began conducting aptitude and achievement testing in its own headquarters, and failed to renew funding for the secretarial training program. In the single remaining vocational training program (electronics), the entrance requirements (in the form of minimum scores on achievement tests in math and reading) were substantially increased. The commission, however, markedly increased the funding for the job placement program, a two-week program which was pragmatically noneducational; it assisted clients in the preparation of resumés and then required them to contact a minimum of fifteen potential employers per week, thus increasing the odds of a successful contact without incurring the costs of skill improvement. The college was at once intensely unhappy and completely powerless to do anything but complain.

The commission's decisions had three major outcomes. First and foremost, it had the dramatic effect of a chess player's discovered check—in a single stroke, the true balance of power was revealed. The commission's move forced the realization upon the college, and upon the center's advisory committee, that the center was not the solid operation it had appeared to be and that without commission funds, the center would simply cease to exist. The college, as operator of the center, had sacrificed any autonomy it could have achieved by allowing itself to become overdependent on a single funding source. Linkages involving the exchange of money are the most dangerous, since, when push comes to shove, decision-making power resides at the funding source. As long as the goals of both agencies are perfectly compatible, the issue might not arise. Agency goals change, however, and in the Commission's case that change took the form of de-emphasizing education and stressing inexpensive job placements.

The second outcome, a direct response to the first, was the warping of the center's original mission. Education, which was and should have been the college's major function, now played a relatively minor role in college-operated center programs. College staff, many of whom were transferred to the job placement program from the eliminated educational programs, no longer served as educators, but as resumé writers, telephone coaches, job developers, and employment counselors. These staff members were confused, and in some cases unable to fill their new roles competently—roles which suited neither their inclinations nor their training. In many cases, they found it difficult to reconcile their personal professional goals (the education of disadvantaged adults) with the center's new mission (rapid job placement).

The third outcome, and a logical outgrowth of the others, was a radical shift in the way the community viewed the center. During the first two years, word had spread through the community that the center had something for everyone regardless of academic proficiency. Now, potential participants were systematically turned away. The stiff entrance requirements for the electronics program, coupled with its limited enrollment capacity, made admission highly competitive, and thus out of the reach of the least educated and most-in-need residents of Crawford. The job placement program accepted only applicants with demonstrated academic proficiency, a solid work history, and the willingness and ability to travel to jobs anywhere within a ten mile radius of Crawford. In effect, the program accepted applicants who were already so qualified that they probably could have found work on their own. The center was no longer serving the people it set out to serve and was no longer a viable force in the development of Crawford's human resources.

The failed collaboration with the Manpower Commission was

unquestionably the most devastating in the center's history and, ultimately, resulted in the undoing of the entire operation. The blame for the failure is somewhat difficult to assign, however, for without this collaboration the center would not have come into existence. If the director of the center is guilty of anything, he is guilty of administrative complacency, in that he allowed the program to continue in a state of overdependency on one major funding source. (Funds from other government agencies totalled about one third of the Manpower Commission allocation.) Efforts to seek other funding sources, particularly corporation and foundation grants, were repeatedly encouraged by the university representative on the advisory board, but they never got beyond the planning stage. Continued Manpower Commission support was considered stable and to be used at the college's discretion — until dramatically shown to be otherwise.

Never-Begotten Collaborations. It is difficult to state categorically that a missed opportunity for collaboration is a mistake, since the consequences remain unknown. In the light of the failed attempts at collaboration described above, one is tempted to believe that the less attempts the center made the better. There were, however, three potential interagency connections that, with hindsight, seem at once so obviously desirable and feasible that they bear mentioning.

The center never established a direct connection with the personnel offices at either of the two major employers in Crawford, Central State University and Croften-Roberts Pharmaceuticals. Together, these two organizations hire hundreds of new employees every year, yet less than a dozen of these jobs went to center participants in the course of four years. Despite the fact that each organization had a representative on the advisory committee, and each had publicly stated that it was committed to the development of Crawford's human resources, no pressure was exerted to make them back up their stated commitment with jobs. The center's job placement program occasionally referred clients to posted job openings in these organizations, but clients were in open competition with other, non-center applicants. No attempt was made to tailor center programs to meet the employee needs of these organizations, and no apprenticeship or work experience programs were instituted, despite federal monies available to do just that.

No cooperative arrangements were made with the other vocational training programs operating in the Crawford area to prepare the college's ABSE students through specialized instruction to enter and succeed in those programs. The center offered only two vocational training options, and together they did not have enough training slots to accommodate the number of applicants. The center referred clients to other programs, but, again, they were in open competition with non-center applicants. The college's ABSE program taught only general basic skills; no attempt was made to focus instruction on the reading and math demands which students would need to qualify for the training programs and to succeed on the job.

Finally, no systematic referral system was established with the other social service agencies that served potential center participants. Flyers were sent to the State Job Service Office and to the Crawford Unemployment Office, but they were never followed up with personal contacts. As a result, few referrals were made, and the center remained dependent on the Manpower Commission for the majority of its learners.

Summary of Failures

The failure of the Crawford Center can, in part, be attributed to certain pecularities in the larger environment. Few cities are as politically volatile as Crawford, and the center quickly became the vortex of powerful and often conflicting forces. Such a situation, however, simply raised the stakes of interagency relationships, making the successful management of collaborations not just a strategy for agency development, but a requisite for agency survival. In the final analysis, the failed collaborations in Crawford can be viewed as the direct and inevitable outcomes of administrative errors, the greatest of which was a nearly obsessive unwillingness to relinquish even a modicum of control. Other administrative errors and oversights are summarized below.

Lack of Candor. Although the director and the dean were right in concluding that the center could not succeed without the support of the local power elites, they were wrong in the way they attempted to gain this support. They were strategically indirect in their dealings with the advisory committee, and by fostering a myth of cosponsorship and joint ownership, they ultimately were forced to suffer the consequences of others' belief in that myth. When the truth gradually emerged, the college lost the support for which it had already sacrificed scarce resources, and was regarded with distrust by the people they had sought to co-opt.

Poor Selection of Partners. In most cases, collaborations were thrust upon the college, and the political stance they had adopted left them without the freedom to decline. With the exception of the Manpower Commission, the college's collaborations resulted from a single-minded quest for a single resource: political support. Other promising collaborations, most notably with local employers and social service agencies, were left uncultivated.

Lack of Planning. The majority of the Crawford failures stem from inadequate planning. Even though the college had relinquished its power to choose its collaborators, the consequences of unwanted collaborations could have been mitigated by negotiating the *details* of the relationship, thus changing the nature of the linkages formed to better serve the development of the center. The failure to properly negotiate collaborations can be attributed to two administrative shortcomings of the director, shortcomings which emerged in virtually every collaborative venture he undertook. First, he seemed to be unaware of the value of his own resources and of which resources he could afford to sacrifice. Second, the director tended to keep the details of a proposed collaboration as vague as possible, presumably to avoid committing himself; this tendency created a situation, however, in which the consequences of the venture were largely unpredictable.

Failure to Implement. The director made several obvious mistakes in respect to implementing collaborations. He repeatedly neglected to inform his staff, not only about such mundane matters as classroom allocation, but about the more important considerations relating to the desired extent of collaboration. For example, when his staff referred students to the Board of Education ABSE program, they believed their actions to be well within the limits of the existing collaboration. Further, once a collaboration had been established, the director simply allowed it to run its course, neglecting to monitor even those collaborations he liked the least. As a result of his passivity, he became aware of problems only when they had reached a crisis point.

Failure to Evaluate. If the director had periodically evaluated the impact of collaborations on center programs, he would have recognized not only that the resources he was sacrificing were not worth the political support he sought, but that, in almost every case, the center simply was not receiving that support. Such a realization might have led to the type of action, either renegotiation or termination of harmful collaborations, which could have saved the center.

Thomas Valentine is the associate director of the Center for Adult Development, Graduate School of Education, Rutgers University.

When the ingredients are right, collaborations work. When they are wrong, collaboration fails and can even be harmful.

Principles for Successful Collaboration

Hal Beder

The descriptions and analyses presented in the four preceding chapters state four dominant themes that explain successful and productive collaborative relationships between continuing education agencies and other organizations: reciprocity, system openness, an atmosphere of trust and commitment, and compatible organizational structure. When the ingredients are right, as in the case of University of Illinois at Chicago's CPE programming (Cervero), collaboration works and the benefits are reaped. When the ingredients are wrong, as they were in the Fingeret and Valentine case studies, collaboration fails and can, in fact, be harmful.

Reciprocity

Although, as Cervero and Beder note, there may be social benefits to collaboration—including reducing competition, avoiding duplication of services, and better coordination of activities—mere exhortations to cooperate generally accomplish little. For collaboration to flourish the parties to it must tangibly benefit, and the key to benefit lies in a reciprocal relationship where both partners to collaboration exchange resources valued less for resources valued more.

Reciprocal benefit is markedly present in the CPE programs of the University of Illinois at Chicago (UIC) and clearly absent from the relationship between Large American University (LAU) and the Public Utility (TPC) described by Fingeret and the Crawford Adult Education Center account presented by Valentine.

UIC collaborated with a multiplicity of organizations in delivering CPE. From these linkages, collaborating organizations received competent instruction, programming expertise, and prestige from being associated with the university. UIC received tangible resources, such as participants and facilities, which, in the long run, were converted into even more valuable intangible resources, such as power, visibility, extension of domain, and legitimacy. That the principle of reciprocity worked is evidenced by the fact that 70 percent of UIC's extension programs are cosponsored, with a cancellation rate at less than one percent.

On the other hand, the university-utility company relationship characterized by Fingeret ultimately failed, as did the Crawford Center studied by Valentine. In the first case, what the university really wanted, research support, was not supplied by the utility; neither was the practical training program desired by the utility supplied by the university. Without reciprocal benefit, the expensive planning effort came to naught.

In the case of Crawford Center, the director's attempts at cooperation were one-way. Although he was willing to take through collaboration, he was not willing to give in any meaningful way. The center's unwillingness to give was played out on two dimensions. In respect to the first, although the director did, in fact, exchange resources with his collaborating partners, he tended to give only that which was expedient. As a result, the collaboration became unbalanced. The center benefitted more than its partners and gave less; the partners felt duped. The second dimension is more subtle, but equally important; the director was unwilling to relinquish control. Loss of some control is a cost of nearly every collaborative relationship. It is a cost that must be borne to obtain the benefits. Failure to include partners in decisions affecting the collaboration and failure to listen to their complaints contributed to perceptions of being duped. Eventually collaboration was terminated.

The lesson is clear: To establish a productive program of collaboration a continuing education agency must (1) identify valued resources it desires to acquire from the environment, (2) identify compatible partners that can supply these resources and that need resources the continuing education program is willing to exchange, and (3) consummate the relationship.

System Openness

All organizations establish boundaries which are more or less permeable. Closed organizations, the C.I.A., for example, have less permeable boundaries in order to restrict unwanted inputs, while open organizations relax their boundaries to permit as many inputs as possible.

Constrasts between the UIC, LAU-TPC, and the Crawford Adult Education Center demonstrate the critical importance of system openness in regard to collaboration. UIC is a very open system receptive to inputs from any health care provider other than its direct competitors. Its repertoire of collaboration includes numerous referral relationships and cosponsorships that range from the United Nations to small community clinics. Its staff sits on the boards of many community and professional organizations. Quoting the director, "There's not a program we provide that doesn't have at least one of these linkages." UIC is more than receptive to outside inputs; it actively seeks them.

The faculty of LAU as portrayed by Fingeret are at the opposite extreme, however. Fearful that the relationship with TPC, the utility company, would affect their curricula, research efforts, and status, they kept the utility at a distance, hearing perhaps what they wanted to hear and ignoring the rest. The result was a proposal for a program that the utility did not want and that it ultimately refused to accept.

While the Crawford Center gave the appearance of being open, in actuality it was not. Input, in the form of advice and requests to cooperate from Central State University, Hispanic groups, and others, was heard but then ignored. In the end, no one bothered any more.

Trust and Commitment

The three case studies make it clear that not only must there be reciprocal benefit, but that also an atmosphere of genuine trust and commitment must prevail for substantial collaboration to occur. UIC's commitment to collaborative efforts is expressed in the director's hope that "every health professional in Illinois would look toward the University of Illinois as the most legitimate provider of CPE."

Trust and commitment are weaker in the two cases representing failures. The utility company studied by Fingeret suspected that the university was more interested in research money than developing a curriculum, and the faculty were not sufficiently concerned with the practical learning needs of the employees. The candid communication that might have resulted in the solution of problems was thus curtailed. Likewise, university faculty did not respect the utility's ability to assess its own learning needs.

In Crawford's case, the center's tendency to put forth positive public relations information while ignoring or burying substantial problems gradually eroded trust and confidence among its supporters on the advisory council and in the community. Potential collaborators shied away.

Trust and commitment derive from at least two factors: the style and personality of key actors in the collaboration and differences in organizational culture. The two are frequently related. For example, it is clear from his statements that the Dean of Continuing Professional Education at UIC had adopted a very open administrative style that resulted in a flexible and receptive organizational culture. His own philosophy of trust and commitment to collaboration pervaded the entire enterprise.

In contrast, however, Crawford Center's director adopted a closed administrative style resulting in a failure to share information and decision making. Initial trust vanished among collaborators who eventually abandoned the relationship.

Perhaps the LAU/TPC relationship best demonstrates the problem of organizational culture clash and its effect on trust and commitment. Universities possess organizational cultures that differ dramatically from industries'. While industries are organized according to a bureaucratic model where authority is hierarchical and motivation is stimulated by extrinsic remuneration, universities are collegial organizations. University faculties operate with great autonomy. The employer has few sanctions to apply to faculty members who are motivated intrinsically by professional values. In effect, universities function more as a federation of independent faculty bound by common professional values than as bureaucratic entities. Both LAU faculty and TPC managers were convinced they were acting approrpiately and in good faith throughout the eventually aborted relationship. Faculty were attempting to protect the integrity of their profession by demanding what they considered to be academic quality. The decision-making process was slow and, from TPC's perspective, loosely organized and inflexible. TPC, on the other hand, was highly pragmatic in its orientation. It wanted trained workers who could do their jobs safely and more efficiently. The professional knowledge base so important to LAU faculty mattered little to managers charged with getting the job done. The two very different organizational cultures clashed. With the clash, trust declined; when trust declined, commitment began to collapse.

Structure

Collaborations are generally more than interpersonal interactions among officials; they usually involve the structures of organizations as well. UIC adopted a highly fluid and flexible organizational structure that permitted it to adapt to the structures of its collaborating partners. This is less true for Crawford Center and decidedly not the case for LAU.

In the case of Crawford Center, the dean of continuing education for Sandoe Community College, which held the center's lease, was frequently caught in a structural problem which was never resolved. Although the college was the legal grantee, the funding organizations represented on the advisory committee felt a sense of ownership. To whom was she responsible — the college that employed her or the founding partners? The two structures mixed poorly. The college desired the center to serve its ends while the advisory council and cooperating partners were more concerned with the needs of the community and the building of a truly cooperative program. Caught in the middle, the dean attempted to play it both ways. It did not work. Center staff adopted the position of the college, their employer. As this became clear to the partners to collaboration, they abandoned the cooperative efforts.

The structures of LAU and the utility company were clearly incompatible. Large American University is a professional organization structured to provide education and conduct research. Relations among faculty members are based on collegiality and institutional authority over faculty is weak. In contrast, TPU, the utility, is an industrial concern providing an essential service. It governs its employees through traditional bureaucratic control. Its authority over its employees is strong. So different were the structures and resulting operating styles that the two organizations simply failed to understand each other. Ultimately, accommodation was impossible.

When organizational structures are incompatible, the operations of collaborating partners become disrupted. Internal strain develops and efficiency is sacrificed. To prevent this from occurring, organizations that collaborate effectively generally adopt fluid and flexible structures that can adapt well to those of their partners. Such was the case of UIC. UIC was decentralized; its subunits had the authority to negotiate and consummate collaborations. Faculty who taught CPE courses were typically part-time and could be hired and released as needs demanded.

The LAU/TPC relationship stands in contrast. The collegial structure of LAU was tightly bound by academic values. Governed primarily by tradition, it was inflexible. Similarly, the hierarchical structure of TPC made flexibility difficult and the reassignment of a key manager who possessed the authority to act disrupted commitment within the hierarchy. Had the LAU/TPC relationship been consummated, we would speculate that the collaboration would have strained both structures to the extent that cooperation would have been short-lived. In fact, realization of this potential strain may have been a factor in TPC's decision to terminate the collaboration. In the name of efficiency, TPC may have demanded that the parts of the curriculum it considered to be superfluous be eliminated. Faculty, not used to bureaucratic demand, would have been resentful and unwilling to sacrifice what they considered necessary for academic quality. In the end, differences in structures would have precluded joint decision making and conflict resolution. The relationship would have ended amid an atmosphere of considerable ill will.

Our final summary is brief. Continuing education agencies that have flexible, adaptive structures, adopt a posture of openness to the external enviornment, operate with a sense of commitment that engenders trust, and adhere to the principle of reciprocal benefit will find it easy to establish successful collaborative relationships. Agencies that do not possess these characteristics will find it difficult to collaborate; the few collaborative relationships that do establish will tend to be unsuccessful and even dysfunctional for one or both collaborating partners.

Hal Beder is an associate professor of adult and continuing education, Graduate School of Education, Rutgers University. He also serves as editor of Adult Education Quarterly.

Index

A

Adult Basic Education (ABE), 6-7, 65, 70, 77-78
Adult basic/secondary education (ABSE), 75-77, 78, 79, 81-82, 83
Adult education center: and advisory committee, 70-73; analysis of mismanagement of, 65-83; background on, 65-66; and board of education, 72, 75-77; described, 68-70; failures of, 68-82; and Hispanic alliance, 73-75; and manpower commission, 71, 73, 75, 78-81; and mental health services, 77-78; and missed opportunities, 81-82; ownership of, 71-73; and reciprocity, 86; and structure, 89; summary on, 82-83; and system openness, 87; and trust, 88
Albany, New York, referral in, 6-7
American Academy of Family Practice, 29
American Dental Association, 26
American Hospital Association, 26
American Medical Association, 26
Aquino, J. T., 24, 37
Autonomy: continuing education agencies, 5; costs to, 35-36; and resource security, 33

B

Bach, M. L., 59, 62
Beder, H. W., 1, 3-22, 25, 26, 29, 31, 37, 66, 67, 85-90
Benson, K. J., 27, 37, 54, 62
Berlin, L. S., 37

C

Cervero, R. M., 1, 23-38, 85
Clark, B., 13, 22
Collaboration, exchange and cosponsored types of, 67-68. *See also* Interorganizational cooperation
Competition: drawbacks of, 9; prevalence of, 24; for resources, 31
Comprehensive Education and Training Act (CETA), 8-9
Continuing education agencies, characteristics of, 3-5
Continuing professional education (CPE): agency for, 26-27; background on, 23-25; case study of, 25-36; collaboration in, 23-38; cost/benefit ratio in, 34-36; example of, 9-10; factors encouraging linkages in, 31-34; implications for, 36-37; intangible resources for, 28-29; linkage types in, 29-31; providers of, 23-24; reciprocity in, 86; and structure, 89; success of, 85; and system openness, 87; tangible resources for, 27-28; and trust, 87, 88
Control, as cost of cooperation, 20-21
Control-coordination, in continuing professional education, 30-31
Cooperation. *See* Interorganizational cooperation
Cooperative Extension Service, 7
Cooptation, drawbacks of, 9
Coordination, characteristics of, 7
Cosponsorship: characteristics of, 6; in continuing professional education, 29-30
Craig, R. L., 37
Cullitan, B. J., 58, 59, 63

D

Darkenwald, G. G., 22, 56, 63
Davies, H. M., 24, 37
Deuton, H. R., 41, 63
Dislocation, as cost of cooperation, 19, 36
Domain: as essential resource, 12-13; as factor encouraging linkage, 33; as intangible resource, 28; in university-industry collaboration, 55, 56, 58, 59, 61

Donor-receiver: characteristics of, 7; in continuing professional education, 30; as exchange collaboration, 67

E

Emery, R. E., 4, 22, 54, 63
English-as-a-second language (ESL), 8-9, 16, 19, 65
Environment: characteristics of, and collaboration, 34; enacted, 54, 56

F

Facilities, as tangible resource, 28
Fingeret, A., 1, 39-63, 85, 86, 87
Flexibility, need for, 4-5
Frampton, G. T., Jr., 58, 59, 63

G

Gannella, J. S., 59, 63
General Education Development (GED), 66, 70, 77
Goal displacement, as cost of cooperation, 19
Goal orientation, in continuing professional education, 32-33
Goat's Bay Continuing Education Program, 14-15
Guthrie, R. C., 60, 63

H

Hackley, D., 22
Hohmann, L., 24, 37
Houle, C. O., 23, 24, 37

I

Illinois at Chicago, University of (UIC), continuing professional education at, 25-36, 85-89
Illinois State Dental Society, 32
Information: as essential resource, 11-12; as tangible resource, 27-28
Insecurity, of continuing education agencies, 5
Institute for Nuclear Power Operations (INPO), 39, 40, 46, 48, 49, 52, 57, 59
Instruction, type of, 31-32

Interorganizational cooperation: analysis of, 3-22; benefits of, 24, 35, 85; concepts in, 66-68; and continuing education agency characteristics, 3-5; in continuing professional education, 23-38; costs of, 18-21, 24, 35-36; defined, 6; examples of, 6-7, 8-11, 13, 14-15, 16-17, 18, 19; factors encouraging, 31-34; mismanagement of, 65-83; practical tips on, 17-18; principles of, 9, 15, 17-18, 60-62; rationale for, 5-6; reciprocity in, 15-17, 85-86; resources essential to, 9-15; risk reduction in, 32; steps in, 86; as strategy for success, 7-9; and structure, 89-90; summary on, 21, 36-37; and system openness, 87; themes in, 85-90; theoretical framework for, 25-26; trust and commitment in, 87-88; types of, 6-7, 29-31; university-industry, 39-63

J

Johnson, E. L., 57, 63
Joint Commission on Accreditation of Hospitals, 26
Jointure for Community Adult Education of Central New Jersey, 8-9

K

Knox, A. B., 24, 37

L

Learners: as benefit, 35; as essential resource, 6, 10-11; as tangible resource, 27
Linkages, concept of, 67
Litwak, E., 54, 63
Lusterman, S., 56, 63

M

McNeil, P., 5, 22
Manning, P. R., 25, 37
Millett, J. D., 57, 63
Money: as essential resource, 9-10; as tangible resource, 27
Moses, S., 14, 22

N

Neighborhood Youth Corps, 18
Nowlen, P. N., 24, 37
Nuclear power plant operator training, case study of collaboration for, 39-63
Nuclear Regulatory Commission (NRC), 39, 41, 44, 46, 50, 52, 59

O

Omenn, G. S., 58, 63
Organizations: characteristics of, and collaboration, 34; loosely coupled, 54, 56; placid and turbulent, 4

P

Pake, G. E., 55, 60, 63
Participants. *See* Learners
Peoria District Dental Society, 29
Peterfreund, S., 56, 63
Pfeffer, J., 54, 58, 63
Philips Company, 7
Power: as essential resource, 13-15; as intangible resource, 28-29; and service activities, 58
Prager, D. J., 58, 63
Prestige, as intangible resource, 28

R

Reciprocity, in interorganizational cooperation, 15-17, 85-86
Referral: characteristics of, 6-7; for continuing professional education, 30
Resources: competition for, 31; dependency on, 20-21; essential, 9-15; insecurity of, 3-4; intangible, 28-29; linkages for, 54; security, of, 33-34; tangible, 27-28
Rogovin, M., 58, 59, 63
Rothman, J., 54, 63

S

Salancik, G. R., 54, 58, 63
Schwab, J. J., 57-58, 63
Searle Laboratories, G. D., 29
Seashore, S. E., 8, 22, 54, 63
Shelton, H. R., 37
Smith, F., 25, 29, 37

Sponsoring body, support from, 35
Staff, as essential resource, 11
Stern, M. R., 23, 24, 37
Structure, and interorganizational cooperation, 89-90
Success: components of, 85-90; defined, 7-8; strategy for, 7-9
Suleiman, A., 24, 37
System openness, and interorganizational cooperation, 87

T

Tatel, D. S., 60, 63
Termination, costs of, 36
Terryberry, S., 4, 22
Thornton, R., 59, 62
Time, as cost of cooperation, 18-19
Trist, E. L., 4, 22, 54, 63
Trust, in interorganizational cooperation, 87-88

U

UIC. *See* Illinois at Chicago, University of
United Nations, 33, 87
University-industry collaboration: analysis of case study of, 39-63; assessments of, 51-53; background on, 39-40; beginning, 43-44; conflict in, 47-48; director for, 53; discussion of, 53-60; domain in, 55, 56, 58, 59, 61; education-training conflict in, 56; feasibility study for, 45-48; and industry environment, 59-60; and legitimation of service activities, 58; overview of, 53-55; principles for, 60-62; product in, 57-59; project for, 40-53; proposal for, 45; rationale for, 41-42; and reciprocity, 86; and structure, 89-90; and system openness, 87; teams for, 40-41; trust in, 58-59, 87-88; university analysis of, 45-47; and university environment, 55-57; university report for, 48-51

V

Valentine, T., 1, 65-83, 85, 86
Visibility, as benefit, 35

W

Welfare Incentive Program (WIN), 20–21
World Health Organization, 33

Y

Young, W. H., 32, 37
Younghouse, R. H., 24, 38
Yuchtman, E., 8, 22, 54, 63

Z

Zeleznik, C., 59, 63